BOOK OF DEMONS

A 13TH AGE SUPPLEMENT

BY GARETH RYDER-HANRAHAN
AND ROB HEINSOO

13TH AGE IS A FANTASY ROLEPLAYING GAME BY
ROB HEINSOO, JONATHAN TWEET,
LEE MOYER, & AARON MCCONNELL

Pelgrane Press

FIRE OPAL

www.fireopalmedia.com and www.pelgranepress.com

CREDITS

PUBLISHERS
Simon Rogers and Cathriona Tobin

ART DIRECTION
Cathriona Tobin and Rob Heinsoo

LAYOUT
Badger McInnes

AUTHORS
Gareth Ryder-Hanrahan and
Rob Heinsoo

COVER ART
Melissa Gay

ICONS, MONSTER TILES, SPOT ILLOS
Lee Moyer, Aaron McConnell

DEVELOPER
Rob Heinsoo

INTERIOR ART
Agathe Pitié, Lauren Covarrubias,
Rich Longmore, Karolina Węgrzyn,
Christine Griffin, Lee Dawn, Vlada
Monakhova

ADDITIONAL DESIGN
Paul Fanning

PLAYTEST CREDITS
Ariel Weinreich, Caleb Shoemaker, Chuck Dee, Dave Ledvora, Dmitryi Bokk, Durkon, Jason Fryer, Jeffrey Kahrs,
Jonathan Tweet, Marty Lund, Michael Todd, Paul Hughes, Paul Weimer, Rob Lightner, Roland Rogers, Sean
Dawson, Stiwen Parshukov, Thiago Juarez Ribeiro Silva, Tim Baker, Victor Faber, Vlad Tin

TABLE OF

CONTENTS

Introduction

The Empire is demon-haunted.

Demons crawl beneath the skin of the world, clawing at it, trying to break out of their prison. They want to destroy everything. They're everyone's enemy.

The Crusader sees this danger. The Great Gold Wyrm died to save us all from premature destruction. And the Diabolist dances on the edge of the Abyss, stealing power from the demons even as she helps them climb out of the pit.

When demons break through into the world, they carve out hellholes, cursed regions where the alien laws of the Abyss hold sway. Each hellhole brings the world one step close to apocalypse.

Take up your sword or staff, adventurer, and hold back the hosts of Hell!*

*Alternatively, see Chapter One for a new character class who has other ideas about the proper usage of the hosts of Hell.

In This Book

The first chapter is aimed at players and GMs. Chapters Two through Four are pretty much for the GM.

Chapter 1: The Demonologist is a newcomer to the Dragon Empire, a new character class who uses demons and demonic powers but might still be on the side of light. Or at least only plausibly deniably evil! Demonologists devoted to the path of corruption, path of flame, and path of slaughter have different talents, spells, and summoned demons that can make them play as very different characters. Speaking of very different characters, the chapter closes with multiclass options.

Chapter 2: Gamemastering Demons has advice and plot seeds connected to demons, and how to extract maximum fun-juice from their infernal schemes. The lies demons might tell about the cosmos could be so fascinating you'll decide they're not entirely lies . . . The chapter also includes a write-up of the ecology of the hellhole as well as new monster stats for the demons introduced by the demonologist's summoning spells.

Chapter 3: Six Hellholes describes one more than five and one fewer than seven hellholes of varying size and power, from the blighted groves of Ratwood to the world-shattering fury of the Hellgout.

Chapter 4: Citadels of the Icons introduces the Crusader's fortress of First Triumph and provides some impressions of the Diabolist's citadel. Which of the two strongholds holds more demons? The answer isn't clear . . .

Chapter 1

DEMONOLOGIST

There's a new type of magician surfacing in the Dragon Empire who might do something about the Empire's demon problem.

It may not be something good.

OVERVIEW

Fighters, wizards, clerics, and rogues are part of the ongoing story of the world. It's pretty clear that heroes with something like the powers portrayed in many of our player character classes took part in the major events of many past ages.

The demonologists we're presenting in this book are a different story. We're presenting the demonologist class as something extremely new in the world, something that hasn't had time to become a well-understood part of the Dragon Empire. You are of course welcome to disagree, especially as part of what makes one of your campaigns unique. Perhaps demonologists existed in long-buried ages and have returned.

A three-part-collision: The simplest explanation for the sudden emergence of the demonologist in the 13th Age is that the three-part war fought by the Crusader, Diabolist, and Great Gold Wyrm is tearing usable holes in the unwholesome fabric of demonkind. Look closely at the three paths currently accessible to the demonologist and you'll see connections to the three icons. They're not necessarily connections that indicate approval or respect. . .

The Crusader doesn't trust anyone but himself to 'handle' demons, so if you're any type of demonologist, even a demonologist on the path of slaughter, and are not in his positive graces, he probably wants you dead.

The Diabolist was never a demonologist (we think!) and she may resent other mortals carving a slice of her power. Then again, maybe she believes that demonologists are by definition corruptible. Perhaps she's right.

You'd think that the Great Gold Wyrm would be an outright enemy of all demonologists, but he's been fighting in the Abyss a *long* time. Maybe his paladins are more stuck up about who they'll consider as allies than the Wyrm is? Maybe demonologists on the path of flame are helping the Great Gold Wyrm, somehow, whether they know it or not?

Play style: Your experience as a demonologist depends on which path you've chosen. As a devotee of the path of corruption or the path of flame, you'll function somewhat like other spellcasters, preferring to keep allies, or your summoned demon, between you and the enemy. If you've focused on the path of slaughter, you're more likely to carry a serious melee weapon and welcome enemies who seek to engage you as unwilling sacrifices!

Like the druid from *13 True Ways*, this class can be fun for players who like to figure out interesting combos from disparate approaches.

Ability Scores: Most demonologists rely on Charisma for serious spellcasting, backed up by Constitution. Exceptions include tiefling demonologists (see the That's Intelligent class feature on page 9) and slaughter path devotees, who use Strength for some of their basic melee attacks when they're too staggered to use Charisma.

Demonologists gain a +2 class bonus to Charisma or Constitution, as long as it isn't the same ability you increase with your racial bonus.

Races: Humans are the most common demonologists, either for the lure of power, the thirst for knowledge, or to use the mysteries of demons against the forces of the Abyss—and there's definitely nothing that can go wrong with motivations like that. Other demonologist stereotypes include half-elves who feel like outsiders, unbalanced gnomes who think demonic magic is funny, and half-orcs and dragonics who embrace the path of slaughter as a way of surprising musclebound rivals.

Of course we have saved the best for last. Some people call tieflings 'the demontouched,' and there's no denying that the race has a natural affinity for all three paths.

Backgrounds: Possible demonologist backgrounds are those that explain how you were driven to learn about demons, or those that aid and conceal your activities, such as: escaped sacrifice, child of cultists, survivor of a demon attack, survivor of a Crusader attack, born of a hellhole, former clergy for the gods of light, once-promising student at a Horizon college, decorated soldier, Axis firefighter, respected doctor at an Imperial hospital, resurrected ancient hero, demon-child.

GEAR

At 1st level, demonologists from different walks of life might start with an incredibly diverse set of possessions. Use ideas from all our other write-ups as you like!

ARMOR

Corruption and flame path demonologists wear light armor made of padding and leather, if they wear armor at all. Slaughter path demonologist wear heavier armor, often at least partially made of demonic carapaces or other shells. Slaughter path armor modifiers appear in the Path of Slaughter section on page 26.

Demonologist Armor and AC

Type	Base AC	Attack Penalty
None	10	—
Light	11	—
Heavy	12	−5
Shield	+1	−2

WEAPONS

Corruption path and flame path demonologists aren't melee warriors. They're better off skulking in the back with a sacrificial dagger or a rune staff. Slaughter path demonologists are more often built for melee, and their weapons show that.

The information in this section applies to most demonologists oriented toward the corruption and flame paths. But slaughter path devotees handle melee much differently; see their feature and talent section for modifications to the stats below.

Demonologist Melee Weapons

	One-Handed	Two-Handed
Small	1d4 dagger	1d6 (−2 atk) club, staff
Light or Simple	1d6 mace, axe, wavy dagger	1d8 (−2 atk) spear
Heavy or Martial	1d8 (−2 atk) longsword, flail	1d10 (−3 atk) greataxe, greatsword

Demonologist Ranged Weapons

	Thrown	Crossbow	Bow
Small	1d4 dagger	1d4 (−2 atk) hand crossbow	—
Light or Simple	1d6 (−2 atk) javelin, axe	1d6 (−2 atk) light crossbow	1d6 (−2 atk) shortbow
Heavy or Martial	—	1d8 (−3 atk) heavy crossbow	1d8 (−3 atk) longbow

BASIC ATTACKS

MELEE ATTACK
At-Will
Target: One enemy
Attack: Strength + Level vs. AC
Hit: WEAPON + Strength damage
Miss: —

RANGED ATTACK
At-Will
Target: One enemy
Attack: Dexterity + Level vs. AC
Hit: WEAPON + Dexterity damage
Miss: —

DEMONOLOGIST LEVEL PROGRESSION

Unlike most other classes, demonologist spells and powers depend on which path the chosen talents belong to. Each path has its own level progression chart detailing the number of spells you'll choose to know each day.

Note: Although not listed on the table, this class gets three talents. It does not gain more talents at higher levels.

Demonologist Level	Total Hit Points*	Total Feats	Level-up Ability Bonuses	Damage Bonus From Ability Score
Level 1 Multiclass	(Avg. of both classes) x **3**	As 1st level PC	Not affected	ability modifier
Level 1	(6 + CON mod) x **3**	1 adventurer		ability modifier
Level 2	(6 + CON mod) x **4**	2 adventurer		ability modifier
Level 3	(6 + CON mod) x **5**	3 adventurer		ability modifier
Level 4	(6 + CON mod) x **6**	4 adventurer	+1 to 3 abilities	ability modifier
Level 5	(6 + CON mod) x **8**	4 adventurer 1 champion		2 x ability modifier
Level 6	(6 + CON mod) x **10**	4 adventurer 2 champion		2 x ability modifier
Level 7	(6 + CON mod) x **12**	4 adventurer 3 champion	+1 to 3 abilities	2 x ability modifier
Level 8	(6 + CON mod) x **16**	4 adventurer 3 champion 1 epic		3 x ability modifier
Level 9	(6 + CON mod) x **20**	4 adventurer 3 champion 2 epic		3 x ability modifier
Level 10	(6 + CO N mod) x **24**	4 adventurer 3 champion 3 epic	+1 to 3 abilities	3 x ability modifier

DEMONOLOGIST STATS

Initiative, AC, PD, MD, Hit Points, Recovery Dice, and Feats are level dependent.

Ability Bonus	+2 Constitution or Charisma (different from racial bonus)
Initiative	Dex mod + Level
Armor Class (light armor)	11 + middle mod of Con/Dex/Wis + Level
Physical Defense	11 + middle mod of Str/Con/Dex + Level
Mental Defense	11 + middle mod of Int/Wis/Cha + Level
Hit Points	(6 + Con mod) x Level modifier (see level progression chart)
Recoveries	(probably) 8
Recovery Dice	(1d6 x Level) + Con mod
Backgrounds	8 points, max 5 in any one background
Icon Relationships	3 (4 at 5th level; 5 at 8th level)
Talents	3
Feats	1 per Level

CLASS FEATURES

In addition to the class features all demonologists have in common, each of the three devotee paths has its own features for initiates and devotees. You'll find the additional corruption path features on page 12, flame path features on page 19, and slaughter path features on page 26.

Features in common for all demonologists follow.

THAT'S INTELLIGENT

Tieflings can use their Intelligence ability score in place of all references to Charisma in demonologist class features, powers, feats, spells, and so on.

You might think that truly intelligent members of other races know better than to be demonologists, but for tieflings it's a logical development. If they handle it right, they can even give the Diabolist a black eye while messing with powers she'd rather have for herself.

INITIATE, DEVOTEE, FANATIC

Like many other classes, you have three talents to choose as a demonologist. Unlike other classes, your talents are grouped within three paths: the path of corruption, path of flame, and path of slaughter. If you choose a single talent from a path, you are an initiate of that path. If you choose two talents from a path, you are a devotee of that path. If you choose all three talents from a single path, you're a fanatic of that path.

The druid in *13 True Ways* has a somewhat similar class structure. But it's only similar, not the same. If the demonologist worked like the druid, you would invest one to three talents in a path to unlock the features of that path. Instead, you're choosing specific varied talents that are each part of an overarching path.

For example, if you take the Contagion and Inimical talents from the corruption path and the Demonic Reinforcements talent from the slaughter path, you are a devotee of corruption and an initiate of slaughter. If you switched one of your corruption path talents out for Flickering from the path of flame, you'd be an initiate of all three paths. If you replaced Demonic Reinforcements with a third corruption path talent, like Misery, you'd be a corruption path fanatic.

Initiates: Initiates gain access to a certain number of powers and spells. They gain access to the path's demon summoning spell as a daily spell, but demons they summon from the path will have fewer hit points than those summoned by devotees and fanatics. The lower hit point numbers for demons summoned by initiates appear in the summoned monster stats.

Initiates also tend to gain a small defense bonus or a small amount of resistance, elements that improved markedly for devotees and fanatics.

Devotees: Devotees gain more access to powers and spells from their path and have the path's bonus demon summoning spell as a recharge 16+ spell. As you'll see, there are also many spells and feats that include devotee bonuses.

Fanatics: You can focus all three talents in one path if you like. As a fanatic, you get an extra spell from your path each day, and your demon summoning spell becomes a recharge 11+ spell instead of recharge 16+. That's probably not as much spellcasting

as you'd gain by being an initiate in a different path, but synergies, character concept, and a slightly more reliable summoning spell may mean it's a good choice.

Some powers and spells specify that they work even better for fanatics, but in most cases, they merely share the advantages enjoyed by devotees. We're choosing not to spell that out every time by writing "devotees and fanatics" whenever there's a devotee advantage. Just remember that powers and bonuses that apply to devotees of a path also apply to fanatics of that path.

Drawbacks

The demonologist weaves a line between raw power and flaws that put it or its allies at risk. You'll soon notice that it's not easy to get rid of those drawbacks—feats that would eliminate a drawback for another class slightly reduce the problem for the demonologist. That's intentional: when you dance with demons, someone is going to get burned.

CHOICE OF IMPLEMENTS

Some demonologists use holy symbols and staffs like clerics, casting spells that qualify as divine magic. Perhaps that should read *unholy* symbols in the demonologists' case, but you get the point. Other demonologists cast arcane spells using the same implements as wizards and sorcerers: wands and staffs. Choose which type of magic you're using when you create your demonologist. As a rule, you don't use both, but perhaps your One Unique Thing breaks the rule.

CURSE SPELLS

Some of the demonologist's spells create curses that wait to be triggered by an enemy. The corruption path is full of such spells, the fire and slaughter paths have a few as well. Unless otherwise specified curse spells are like most other spells: they require a standard action to cast. Others only require a quick action.

Unlike other spells, curse spells don't have an immediate impact, their full effect waits to be triggered by something that's outs of the caster's control, usually a specific enemy natural attack roll or some other specific d20 roll.

Most curses require you to use an interrupt action to take effect when triggered. The enemy's roll triggers the possibility for the curse you have already set in motion by casting a spell on your turn, but the curse doesn't take effect unless you also use an interrupt action to finish the job.

Unless otherwise specified, a spell's curse effect is expended when used.

One curse per roll: The major limitation on curse effects is that a specific d20 roll can trigger only one curse spell per demonologist. For example, if you have cast both *curse of the odd* and *whipping tongues of fire*, you'll choose one of the two to trigger the next time an enemy has a natural odd attack roll.

If there are two demonologists in a group, the same d20 roll could trigger one curse from each of them. Decide on whether or not you trigger a curse in initiative order.

Time limits: Like most other spells and powers, curse effects end at the end of a battle, though they might still linger if the GM pushed the party into another battle without giving them a quick rest.

If the GM feels permissive and the demonologist believes they are about to enter combat—say, when about to open a door into the monsters' guard room—it might be OK to cast a curse spell first, but a curse waiting to be triggered eliminates any chance for surprise. Curses are a non-subtle ugly feeling that's something bad is about to happen.

Other Paths

One of the side effects of our path-based approach to the demonologist class is that the class could be expanded someday. Creating a fourth demonologist path isn't something we're planning, but let us know if you see another demonologist path that's begging to be unsealed.

Demon Summoner

If you have played other summoning characters, the mechanics of demonologist summoning are more like the druid and necromancer summoning in *13 True Ways* than the wizard summoning in the *Summoning Spells* issue of 13th Age Monthly and the earth priestess and hell mother summoning in *13th Age Glorantha*. Most significantly, as a demonologist, you get superior summoned creatures that don't require you to spend actions to control them.

Good news, bad news: The good news is that we can skip all the rules that apply to creatures that have to be controlled by their summoner's actions.

The bad news is that your summoned demon has a half-life, because every demon summoned by a demonologist takes special ongoing damage called degradation that can't be saved against or stopped!

Degradation: Each of the demonologist's summoned demons has its own degradation statistic, usually expressed as something like this: "At the end of each of its turns, the summoned [demon] suffers 2d6 damage." If you and your GM want to cut down on die rolls, use the average result . . . but rolling at the end of each of your demons' turns is more in the spirit of the class.

Effects that end conditions can't affect degradation. Nor can effects that move conditions around between creatures— degradation is an ability that can't be moved off a summoned demon or copied onto another creature. Your summoned demon is stuck taking its degradation damage until it drops to 0 hit points, and will continue to take that damage if you lose control of it.

Degradation damage continues even when battles are over, but once a battle is over you can dismiss your demon with a quick action. Not before!

Loss of control: Remember how we said you don't have to use actions to control your demon, the way wizards and earth priestesses do? The bad news is that when your summoned demons drop to 0 hit points, there's a chance they're actually breaking free of your control and are about to become fanatic enemies.

Roll an easy save (6+) whenever one of your summoned demons drops to 0 hit points. Bump that save up by 5 points if you are unconscious at the time; in other words, probably a normal save (11+). But for each summoned demon you have in play at that moment, bump the save up another 5 points. To take an unlikely but mathematically interesting example, if you somehow managed to summon three demons at the same time, and are conscious, the control save when a demon drops to 0 hit points will be effectively a hard save, 16+. If you're unconscious when one of your three demons goes down, the necessary save will be 21+, something you'll only succeed on by rolling a natural 20 or having save bonuses.

If the save succeeds, no problem, the demon is dead and banished. If the save fails, the demon gains hit points equal to its staggered value plus its level. It's no longer in your control and is now an enemy! By preference it attacks its former summoner, but it may fight somewhat intelligently to do as much sadistic harm as possible to the summoner and their allies. We play that the demonologist's player has to roll for their out-of-control demon's attacks using their lucky d20, but maybe you're more forgiving than us.

The degradation damage the demon has been suffering from in the battle continues. When the out of control demon finally drops to 0 hit points again, it's eliminated.

Enemies, allies, and out of control demons: Out of control demons usually aren't allies of the player characters' other enemies, but an out of control demon isn't interested in helping its summoner by fighting their enemies. Creatures that aren't smart or evil enough to notice and take advantage of that may still target the out of control demon, but the demon will focus on its true enemies.

No healing: Unlike other summoned creatures, demons summoned by demonologists can't heal.

Adventurer Feat: You have a +1 bonus to the save to avoid losing control of your summoned demons when they drop to 0 hit points.

Champion Feat: Demons you summon can be placed nearby you instead of next to you.

Epic Feat: You gain a +4 attack and defense bonuses against demons you summoned that are now out of control. (Unless they're extremely angry with you, demons understand that you're a tougher target and are more likely to attack your allies.)

Summoning Rules

These new summoning rules are not meant to be used with the druid and necromancer class from *13 True Ways*. Those classes have their own power ecosystem that doesn't integrate with the general rules below.

The all caps tags about elements that have been CHANGED are for people who have played with summoning spells as they were introduced in *13th Age Monthly* and in *13 True Ways*. If you're all caught up with the latest versions of summoning rules as they appear in *13th Age Glorantha*, you'll only need to take special note of the NEW paragraphs below, which mention ways that these summoned demons diverge from standard summoning rules.

Standard action spells: Casting a summoning spell generally requires a standard action. The creature(s) you summon appears next to you, though feats or powers might enable you to summon it nearby instead.

Four types (CHANGED): There are four types of summoned creature, but the demons you summon are all *superior* creatures. Superior creatures take their turns like any other creature without needing to be controlled.

Duration & death damage (CHANGED, NEW): A summoned creature fights for you until the end of the battle, until it is dismissed, or until it drops to 0 hit points. Other classes suffer damage when their summoned creatures drop to 0 hp, but you don't: we've already gone into your control problems above!

And yes, your summoned demon still fights for you if you've been dropped to 0 hit points and are unconscious, but as mentioned above, the save when the demon drops to 0 hit points is tougher if you are unconscious yourself.)

Action economy: The turn you summon it, your demon takes its turn immediately after your turn in initiative order. The summoned creature continues to take its turn immediately after you (even if your initiative order changes) until the end of the battle.

Simpler timing (CHANGED): Having summoned creatures take their turn immediately after their summoner is the mechanically correct way to handle the timing. But in practice, we notice that hardly anyone wants to play that way. Most players want to mix their summoned creature's actions in during their character's turn. If you want to fudge the timing and allow this, it's almost always fine. So our simpler rule is that you can mix the actions together if you want, but if the GM decides it's confusing or the rules are starting to have conflicts, the GM can enforce the 'proper' turn order.

Superior creatures' actions: During its turn, a superior creature can act like any other creature, taking a standard, move, and quick action.

Dismissal (NEW): Like most other summoners, you can dismiss your summoned creature using a quick action. However, dismissing a demon during combat isn't that simple: after dismissing the demon, roll a control save as if the demon had dropped to 0 hit points. If the demon goes out of control, use its current hit points or the amount it would have if it dropped to 0 and then went out of control, whichever is higher.

Out of combat you concentrate fully and dismiss your summoned demon without rolling a control save.

Hit points: Each summoned creature stat block indicates its base hit points. Starting hit points for summoned creatures are nearly always lower than hit points for non-summoned versions of the same creature. Some class feats might increase the hit points of summoned creatures.

Attack bonuses (CHANGED): Summoned creatures use the default bonuses of their summoner's magic weapon or implement, if any. In other words, if you have an attack and damage bonus from a magic weapon or implement, so do any creatures you summon.

Defense bonuses (CHANGED): Similarly, summoned creatures use the default bonuses of their summoner's armor, cloak, and and head items, if any. In other words, default bonuses to AC, PD, and MD from magic items also apply to your summoned creatures.

As with the attack bonuses covered above, this only applies to default bonuses. Bonuses and abilities that come along with an item that are not default bonuses only apply to summoned creatures if they specify that. At present, not many do.

Escalation die (CHANGED): Summoned creatures use the escalation die. There are creatures summoned by the druid and necromancer that don't, but your demons do.

Allies? (CHANGED): Summoned creatures generally count as your allies, but you can choose to treat them as non-allies when that's better for you. For example, when a monster's attack is against one of its random enemies, it's good for you to have your summoned creature count as an ally of yours and an enemy of the monster. But take the case of the bard's 3rd level spell, *wild heal*. Odds are the bard PC in your group doesn't want to have to include your summoned creature as one of the random allies that might get to heal, so they can choose to ignore your summoned creature as an ally.

A corollary to this is that if PCs have spells or effects that count the *number* of allies, count all creatures summoned by a single PC as a single additional ally. This isn't a hugely important rule, but if it comes up in some weird corner cases, it's sitting here in case the GM wants to prevent tacky abuses.

No nastier specials: If a creature you're summoning sometimes has nastier specials when it appears as a monster, that's not the version of the creature you're summoning ... unless you create a story with the GM explaining why this *one* time you have managed to summon the powerful version of the creature that has the nastier special.

Spell or creature?: When a summoning spell is cast, it's definitely a spell. After casting the spell, a summoned creature is a creature, though if the GM is feeling puckish they might allow effects that generally only interact with spells to interact with a summoned creature. That seems dicey, but it's possible.

Ritual Magic

You can cast your spells as rituals. Demonologist rituals tend to horrify other magicians. That could be for dramatic effect, or it could be an important element of your seriously twisted magic.

DEMONOLOGIST TALENTS

Each of your talents belongs to one of three demonic paths: the path of corruption, the path of fire, or the path of slaughter.

Choosing a single talent from a path unlocks spells and powers that are not available to characters who are not initiated onto that path. Demonologists who choose a second talent from path are devotees. A third talent from a path makes you a fanatic. Devotees and fanatics gain greater powers and spells than initiates.

We're presenting the three demonologist paths as separate micro-classes, similar to our handling of the druid. The paths are meant to mix, but the talents and the spells they unlock are simpler to parse when presented one path at a time.

We'll start with the talents, bonus summoning spell, and full spell list for the path of corruption. The path of flame comes next on page 19, followed by the path of slaughter on page 26. You'll probably want to skim through the talents for each of the paths before designing your first demonologist.

Path of Corruption

Poison, plague, contagion, weakness, confusion, and madness: these are a few of your favorite things.

Resist poison power

Corruption **initiates** gain resist poison 12+, taking half damage from poison attacks unless the attack's natural attack roll is 12+

For corruption path **devotees**, the power increases to resist poison 14+.

For corruption path **fanatics**, the power increases to resist poison 16+.

Interrupt Actions

The demonologist has a number of spells and talent-based powers that use interrupt actions. If it has been awhile since you read the details of the various types of actions on page 162 of the core *13th Age* rulebook, you can use one interrupt action when it's not your turn, but you can't use another interrupt action until the end of your next turn. Depending on the talents and spells you choose, there may well be times you decide to skip using a possible interrupt action, hoping for a better opportunity before your next turn.

Ignore poison resistance

Corruption path **initiates** ignore *resist poison 14+* or lower.

Corruption path **devotees** ignore *resist poison 16+* and lower.

Corruption path **fanatics** ignore *resist poison 18+* and lower.

Bonus summoning spell

Corruption **initiates** gain *summon corruption demon* as a daily spell.

Corruption path **devotees** instead have *summon corruption demon* as a recharge 16+ spell.

Corruption path **fanatics** instead have *summon corruption demon* as a recharge 11+ spell.

Corruption Path Talents

Contagion

You can use this power a number of times per day equal to your Constitution modifier (or 1, if your demonologist has low Constitution).

When an enemy suffering from a save ends effect (including ongoing damage) or a save ends condition caused by one of your demonologist spells drops to 0 hit points, transfer that save ends spell effect or condition to a different nearby enemy with 90 hit points or fewer as an interrupt action. (Contagion only applies to effects created your spells, not your summoned creatures.)

The save required for the new enemy to end the effect decreases; a hard save becomes a normal save, a normal save becomes an easy save, and an easy save stays as an easy save.

2nd level demonologist	110 hit points or fewer
3rd level demonologist	150 hit points or fewer
4th level demonologist	188 hit points or fewer
5th level demonologist	230 hit points or fewer
6th level demonologist	300 hit points or fewer
7th level demonologist	380 hit points or fewer
8th level demonologist	450 hit points or fewer
9th level demonologist	600 hit points or fewer
10th level demonologist	750 hit points or fewer

Adventurer Feat: Once per battle, if you are conscious when the escalation die reaches 5+, gain another use of the Contagion power that day.

Champion Feat: Saves required against spell effects that you have moved using this talent no longer decrease; a hard save stays hard, a normal save stays normal.

Epic Feat: Moving a condition with the Contagion power is a free action for you rather than an interrupt action, so you're not limited to using it once per round.

Contagion Details

First, it's worth noting that Contagion doesn't apply to effects created by your summoned creatures. Second, Contagion moves effects that the target was suffering from before the attack that drops it to 0 hit points. You can't eliminate a target that wasn't suffering from any of your spell effects with a spell and transfer anything, even if that attack spell would have created a condition if the target had survived.

Corrupt Beyond Degradation

You gain a +2 bonus to MD and *resist 16+ psychic damage.*

Adventurer Feat: If you have at least one relationship point with the Diabolist, you roll saves against conditions caused by attacks against MD at the start of your turn instead of the end of your turn.

Champion Feat: When an enemy rolls a natural odd attack roll against your MD, they take psychic damage equal to the attack roll. Increase this damage to double the attack roll at 8th level.

Epic Feat: You gain a +2 bonus to death saves.

Inimical

Enemy saves against effects created by spells you cast are more difficult. Easy saves require a 7+, normal saves require a 12+, and hard saves require a 17+.

Adventurer Feat: If you are a corruption path devotee, twice per day as a free action, you can choose a condition created by an ally's spell to gain the increase in saving throw difficulty you'd get from Inimical.

Champion Feat: You're even more inimical than most. Your spells' easy saves require an 8+, your normal saves require a 13+, and your hard saves still require a 17+ (that's hard enough).

Epic Feat: Once per battle, force an enemy to reroll a save that has been affected by this talent.

Infernal Familiar

You have an infernal familiar, much like a wizard's familiar (core *13th Age* rulebook p. 149). Infernal familiars are usually imps of some description, but might also take the form of toads, bats, insects, talking skulls, living flames, animated tattoos, sinister oil paintings, or your own eerie shadow.

Use the rules for the Wizard's Familiar with the following modifications.

Infernal familiars are always **Talkative** and possess one other power of your choice from those available to familiars on page 150 of the *13th Age* core rulebook, except that **Tough** is off-limits; demonologist's familiars aren't tough—no easy +1 save bonus for you. **Flight** is a popular option, unless those impish wings are just for show.

Other familiar powers you can choose from for you infernal familiar include:

Blighty: When you heal using a recovery, deal damage equal to your level to an enemy engaged with you. If there are no enemies engaged with you, deal the damage to a random nearby enemy.

Diabolic: If you have one or more relationship points with the Diabolist, you gain a +1 bonus to all your defenses against attacks by demons. *Maybe* devils, also, if that fits the story of your campaign at this tier. This advantage may be represented by having a familiar that chats familiarly with demons, regardless of whether or not you're fighting those demons. That's a special effect that should supply the GM with story hooks and you with occasional bits of unexpected information.

Misery

The first time each round that a nearby non-mook enemy fails a save, deal psychic damage equal to your Constitution modifier to a different nearby enemy. At 5th level, the damage increases to double your Constitution modifier. At 8th level, triple your Con mod.

Adventurer Feat: The enemy that takes the psychic damage can now be far away instead of nearby.

Champion Feat: Two battles per day, you deal Misery damage to a nearby enemy the first time each round that anyone else in the battle, enemy or ally, fails a save.

Epic Feat: As the champion feat, but every battle instead of two battles a day.

CORRUPTION PATH LEVEL PROGRESSION

Demonologist Level	Corruption Initiate Spells	Corruption Devotee Spells	Corruption Fanatic Spells	Spell Level
Level 1 Multiclass	*1*	*1*	*2*	*1st level*
Level 1	1	2	3	1st level
Level 2	1	3	4	1st level
Level 3	2	3	4	3rd level
Level 4	2	4	5	3rd level
Level 5	2	5	6	5th level
Level 6	3	5	6	5th level
Level 7	3	6	7	7th level
Level 8	3	6	7	7th level
Level 9	3	7	8	9th level
Level 10	3	7	8	9th level

CORRUPTION BONUS SPELL

Corruption initiates gain summon corruption demon as a daily spell (as explained in the class features above).

Corruption path **devotees** instead have summon corruption demon as a recharge 16+ spell.

Corruption path **fanatics** have summon corruption demon as a recharge 11+ spell.

This bonus spell is not counted against the spells you choose from according to your level progression.

SUMMON CORRUPTION DEMON

Ranged Spell

Usage depends on talents in path

Effect: You summon a demon to fight for you until the end of the battle as a superior (but degrading!) summoned creature. The demon summoned is determined by the level you cast the spell at, as follows:

1st level spell	summon hopping toad
3rd level spell	summon hopping imp
5th level spell	summon vulture demon
7th level spell	summon hezrou
9th level spell	summon boar demon

SUMMONED DEMON TOAD

1st level spoiler [DEMON]

Initiative: +3

Toothy bite +6 vs AC—4 damage

C: Foul belch +6 vs. PD (1 random nearby enemy)—6 poison damage, and target is dazed until the end of its next turn.
Limited use: 1d4 times per battle.

Dissssgusting: Attackers that roll a natural odd melee attack roll against the demon toad take 1d6 poison damage

Degradation: At the end of each of its turns, the summoned demon toad suffers 1d10 damage.

AC	15	
PD	14	**HP 36** (Initiate: 30)
MD	11	

SUMMONED HOPPING IMP

3rd level spoiler [DEMON]
Initiative: +7

Festering claws +7 vs. AC—7 damage, and 3 ongoing damage

R: Blight jet +7 vs. PD—7 damage, and the target is dazed *(save ends)*
First natural 16+ each turn: The imp can choose one: the target is weakened instead of dazed; OR the imp can make a blight jet attack against a different target as a free action.

Curse aura: Whenever a creature attacks the imp and rolls a natural 1–5, that creature takes 1d8 psychic damage.

Degradation: At the end of each of its turns, the summoned hopping imp suffers 2d6 damage.

AC	19	
PD	13	HP 40 (Initiate: 33)
MD	15	

SUMMONED VULTURE DEMON

5th level spoiler [DEMON]
Initiative: +8

Filth-covered claws +10 vs. AC (2 attacks)—7 damage, and 5 ongoing poison damage
Natural even hit: The vrock can make a demonic screech attack as a free action.

[Special trigger] C: Demonic screech +10 vs. MD (1d3 nearby enemies), 3 psychic damage, and the target is vulnerable *(attacks vs. it have crit range expanded by 2)* until the end of the battle
Limited use: 1d3 times per battle, or any number of times if the vulture demon is out of the demonologist's control.

Degradation: At the end of each of its turns, the summoned vulture demon suffers 4d6 damage.

AC	19	
PD	16	HP 82 (Initiate: 68)
MD	16	

SUMMONED HEZROU

7th level spoiler [DEMON]
Initiative: +10

Meaty, clawed hands +12 vs. AC (2 attacks)—15 damage

Demonic stench: While engaged with this creature, non-demon enemies with 84 hp or fewer are dazed (–4 attack) and do not add the escalation die to their attacks.

Degradation: At the end of each of its turns, the summoned hezrou suffers 4d12 damage.

AC	21	
PD	15	HP 150 (Initiate: 120)
MD	19	

SUMMONED BOAR DEMON

Large 9th level spoiler [DEMON]
Initiative: +12

Musky claw or slimy hoof +14 vs. AC—34 damage
Miss: The nalfeshnee gains a +4 attack bonus until it hits. Unlike most effects, let it stack.

R: Accursed burst +14 vs. PD (1d3 nearby enemies)—34 cold/fire/lightning/negative energy damage (your choice), and the boar demon can make an *abyssal curse* attack as a free action
[Special trigger] Abyssal curse +14 vs. MD (each creature hit by *accursed burst*)—the target is weakened until the end of its next turn
Limited use: 1d3 times per battle, or any number of times if the summoned boar demon is out of the demonologist's control.
Flight: Boar demons are clumsy but powerful fliers with strangely small wings.
Degradation: At the end of each of its turns, the summoned boar demon suffers 5d12 damage.

AC	23	
PD	18	HP 220 (Initiate: 190)
MD	22	

CORRUPTION SPELLS

Now for the rest of the corruption path spells, the spells you'll choose.

1ST LEVEL CORRUPTION SPELLS

CURSE OF THE ODD

Ranged curse spell

Recharge 11+ after battle

Special: This spell creates a curse that's waiting to be triggered by any nearby enemy's natural odd attack roll. Only the first attack roll of a creature on its turn, or the first attack roll in a round by a particular mob of mooks can trigger the curse. When an enemy triggers the curse (and remember, you can only trigger one of your curses per attack roll), make the following attack as an interrupt action.

Target: Enemy that triggered the curse.

Attack: Charisma + Level vs. MD

Hit: 20 psychic damage.

Miss: —

3rd level spell	30 damage
5th level spell	50 damage
7th level spell	80 damage
9th level spell	120 damage

Adventurer Feat: If you're a corruption initiate, *curse of the odd* is now a recharge 6+ spell. If you're a corruption devotee, *curse of the odd* is now a once per battle spell.

Champion Feat: You now deal half damage with *curse of the odd* attacks if you miss.

STAB IN THE SOUL

Ranged spell

At-Will

Target: One nearby enemy

Attack: Charisma + Level vs. MD

Hit: 2d8 + Charisma negative energy damage.

Miss: You take damage equal to the target's level.

3rd level spell	4d8 damage
5th level spell	6d8 damage
7th level spell	9d8 damage
9th level spell	9d12 damage

Adventurer Feat: Add this trigger effect to the attack: *Natural even hit:* As above, and negative energy damage equal to your Constitution modifier (5th level: double your Constitution mod; 8th level: triple) when target misses with an attack (save ends).

Champion Feat: Can now target a far away enemy.

DISEASED BLOOD

Close-quarters spell

Daily for initiates, or **recharge 16+** after the battle for corruption devotees/fanatics

Free action, when a melee attack hits you.

Target: The enemy that hit you (unlike a curse, this does not interrupt their attack, you're attacking after taking the damage).

Attack: Charisma + Level vs. PD

Hit: 4d12 + Charisma poison damage.

Miss: Half damage.

3rd level spell	6d12 damage
5th level spell	6d20 damage
7th level spell	9d20 damage
9th level spell	4d8 x 10 damage

Adventurer Feat: Spell is now recharge 16+ for initiates, recharge 11+ for devotees and fanatics.

Champion Feat: You can cast this spell even if you are unconscious.

Epic Feat: When you take a critical hit in melee, you can cast this spell even if it was already expended.

MINOR CURSE

Ranged curse spell

Recharge 6+ after battle

Quick action to cast

Special: This spell creates a curse that's waiting to be triggered by a nearby enemy's natural 1-5 attack roll. Only the first attack roll of a creature with 60 hit points or fewer, on its turn, or the first attack roll in a round by a particular mob of mooks can trigger this curse. When an enemy triggers the curse, make the following attack as an interrupt action.

Target: Enemy that triggered the curse.

Attack: Charisma + Level vs. MD

Hit: Target is dazed and vulnerable until the end of its next turn.

Hit by 4+: Target is weakened and vulnerable (normal save ends both).

Miss: —

3rd level spell	120 hit points or fewer
5th level spell	200 hit points or fewer
7th level spell	350 hit points or fewer
9th level spell	570 hit points or fewer

Adventurer Feat: Add 30 to the hit point threshold.

Champion Feat: If you are a corruption path devotee, the spell is now a once per battle spell.

Epic Feat: Add another 100 to the hit point threshold.

RABBLE BABBLE

Close spell

Daily, or **recharge 16**+ after the battle for corruption devotees

Target: 1d3 nearby enemies with 30 or fewer maximum hit points, and/or any number of nearby mooks in a mob with printed hit points of 30 or less. (In other words, ignore damage, this only works against targets that start with low hit points.)

Attack: Charisma + Level vs. MD

Hit: The target is confused (save ends).

Miss: The target is confused until the end of its next turn.

3rd level spell	45 hit point threshold
5th level spell	76 hit point threshold
7th level spell	140 hit point threshold
9th level spell	240 hit point threshold

Adventurer Feat: If a creature confused by this spell drops an enemy to 0 hit points, the confusion effect on it continues an additional turn after it would normally end.

Champion Feat: On an even hit, the save to end the confusion is hard (16+).

Epic Feat: Add 60 to the hit point threshold.

SPREADING THE ROT

Ranged spell

Daily, or **recharge 16**+ after the battle for corruption devotees/fanatics

Target: One nearby enemy.

Attack: Charisma + Level vs. PD

Hit: 10 poison damage, and target takes 5 ongoing poison damage; when the target saves against the ongoing damage or drops to 0 hit points, increase the amount of ongoing poison damage to 10 and move the effect to a nearby enemy as a free action. The spell's effect doesn't go beyond this second creature.

Miss: Regain the use of this spell.

3rd level spell	20 damage from the initial hit
5th level spell	30 damage from the initial hit, 10 ongoing that increases to 15 ongoing
7th level spell	40 damage from the initial hit, 20 ongoing that increases to 30 ongoing
9th level spell	70 damage from the initial hit, 30 ongoing that increases to 50 ongoing

Adventurer Feat: Add the current escalation die to the ongoing damage (5th level: double the escalation die; 8th level: triple the escalation die).

Champion Feat: When the spell spreads to a second enemy, it also spreads to a third.

3RD LEVEL CORRUPTION SPELLS

CARRION SCREECH

Close-quarters spell

Daily

Targets: 1d3 nearby enemies

Attack: Charisma + Level vs. MD

Hit: 6d6 + Charisma psychic damage, and the target is vulnerable (save ends)

Miss: Half damage, and the target is vulnerable until the start of your next turn.

5th level spell	10d6 damage
7th level spell	9d10 damage
9th level spell	2d8 x 10 damage

Adventurer Feat: If you are a corruption initiate, this is now a recharge 18+ spell. If you are a corruption devotee, this is now a recharge 16+ spell.

Champion Feat: Spell now targets 1d4 nearby enemies.

Epic Feat: One battle per day, the ongoing poison damage created by the champion feat is accompanied by a hampered effect.

EVEN WORSE CURSE

Ranged curse spell

Recharge 6+ after battle

Special: This spell creates a curse that's waiting to be triggered by a nearby enemy's natural even attack roll. Only the first attack roll of a creature on its turn, or the first attack roll in a round by a particular mob of mooks can trigger the curse. When an enemy triggers the curse (and remember, only one curse can be triggered per attack roll), make the following attack, interrupting their attack.

Target: Enemy that triggered the curse.

Attack: Charisma + Level vs. PD

Hit: 30 negative energy damage.

Miss: 10 damage

5th level spell	50 damage, 15 on a miss
7th level spell	80 damage, 25 on a miss
9th level spell	120 damage, 40 on a miss

MISFORTUNE

Ranged spell

Recharge 6+ after battle

Quick action to cast

Target: One nearby enemy with 70 or less hit points

Attack: Charisma + Level vs. MD

Hit: The target suffers a misfortune (hard save ends, 16+): When the target hits with an odd attack roll, it is a miss instead, and the target gains a +5 bonus (cumulative) to the save against this *misfortune* effect.

5th level spell	100 or less hit points
7th level spell	170 or less hit points
9th level spell	280 or less hit points

Adventurer Feat: On a miss, you regain the use of this spell, though you can't cast it again until a subsequent turn.

Champion Feat: When target misses with a natural odd attack roll, the attack instead targets and hits an ally of theirs engaged with the target, if any, for half damage (no new attack roll, it's an automatic hit). If an enemy is damaged in this fashion, the target gains a +5 bonus (cumulative) to the save against this *misfortune* effect.

Epic Feat: On a natural 1, or when the target misses with an odd attack roll and none of the target's allies are engaged with the target of their attack, the target of this spell somehow hits themselves for half damage. They still get the +5 cumulative bonus to save against this spell.

5TH LEVEL CORRUPTION SPELLS

KILLING DOUBT

Ranged spell

Daily, or **recharge 16+** after the battle for corruption devotees

Interrupt action to cast, when an enemy does something besides move normally or make a basic attack.

Target: One enemy with 160 hp or less

Attack: Charisma + Level vs. MD

Hit: The target loses whatever attack or power triggered this spell (hard save ends).

Miss: The target is dazed until the end of your next turn.

7th level spell	266 HP
9th level spell	400 HP

Champion Feat: On a miss, the target loses whatever attack or power triggered this spell until the start of your next turn.

Epic Feat: A hit also cancels the use of the attack or power that triggered this spell, unless that makes NO sense!

MELTING FLESH

Ranged Spell

Daily

Target: A number of nearby enemies with a total of 160 hp or less, targeting enemies with the fewest hit points first.

Attack: Charisma + Level vs. PD

Hit: 5d8 + Charisma poison damage and the target takes ongoing poison damage equal to triple your Constitution modifier and is stuck and hampered (save ends all)

Miss: Half damage.

7th level spell	250 hit point total, 7d8 damage, ongoing damage equal to quadruple your Constitution modifier
9th level spell	500 hit point total, 10d8 damage, ongoing damage equal to five times your Constitution modifier

Champion Feat: Spell is now recharge 16+.

Epic Feat: Save is now a hard save (16+).

7TH LEVEL CORRUPTION SPELL

ABYSSAL BARGAIN

Ranged Spell

Once per level

Special: You can only cast this spell once on each of your player character allies

Target: One ally at 0 hit points, or that has died since your last turn.

Attack: Charisma + Level vs. MD, or automatic hit against a willing target

Hit: Instead of dying or staying at 0 hit points, the target heals to their staggered hit points, regains consciousness, and loses an icon relationship that's important to them.

The character then gains an ambiguous relationship with an icon of the GM's choice (if they were unwilling), or perhaps a positive one (if they were willing). This can exceed the normal relationship maximums. This isn't necessarily with the Diabolist, but it's probably with the Diabolist, Great Gold Wyrm, or Crusader, whatever will disappoint the newly risen hero the most. And last and most complicated: advantages used with this icon always have complications!

Miss: You regain this spell after your next full heal-up.

GRIEF?

Some playtesters were unhappy with *abyssal bargain's* ability to alter another player's character. If you and your group agree that this is a line that shouldn't be crossed, one simple revision to the spell is to rule that it can only be used against a willing target. We're happier with that variant ourselves. We preserved the harsher variant in case your epic level campaign wants to have things shaken up a bit.

9TH LEVEL CORRUPTION SPELL

HERALD OF APOCALYPSE
Close-quarters spell
Daily
Effect: Until the end of the battle, you can teleport once per round as a move action, provided that you teleport into engagement with a creature you have not already attacked with the attack associated with this spell.
Special: Once per round until the end of the battle, you can use the following attack as a quick action. All ongoing effects that a specific target suffers from the spell are ended by a hard save (16+). The natural odd and natural even effects of the spell may cause a creature to make saves while its hit points are still too high to be fully affected by the spell, but when its hit points drop below the threshold it will suffer the consequences if it hasn't saved.
Close-quarters spell
Target: One engaged enemy you have not already attacked with this spell this battle.
Attack: Charisma + Level vs. MD
Hit: 5d8 + Charisma negative energy damage and the target takes 15 ongoing negative energy damage (hard save ends).
Natural even hit or miss: Target is stuck if it has 600 hit points or fewer (hard save ends).
Natural odd hit or miss: Target is hampered if it has 600 hit points or fewer (hard save ends).
Effect: While making saves from effects created by this spell, an enemy takes a −4 attack penalty against the caster of *herald of apocalypse*, and also deals half damage to the caster.

PATH OF FLAME

It's no surprise that demonologists summon hellfire. The surprise is that some of the magicians on the path of flame seem to have been called to it by the Great Gold Wyrm.

RESIST FIRE POWER
Flame path **initiates** gain resist fire 12+, taking half damage from fire attacks unless the attack's natural attack roll is 12+.
For flame path **devotees**, the power increases to resist fire 14+.
Flame path **fanatics** have resist fire 16+.

IGNORE FIRE RESISTANCE
Flame path **initiates** ignore resist fire 14+ or lower.
Flame path **devotees** ignore resist fire 16+ and lower.
Flame path **fanatics** ignore resist fire 18+ and lower.

BONUS SUMMONING SPELL
Flame **initiates** gain summon flame demon as a daily spell. (The spell appears on page 20.)
Flame path **devotees** instead have summon flame demon as a recharge 16+ spell.
Flame path **fanatics** instead have summon flame demon as a recharge 11+ spell.

FLAME PATH TALENTS

BREATH OF FIRE
You have a breath weapon attack. You can decide whether it seems demonic, draconic, or like something else entirely.

FLAME BREATH
Close-quarters attack
Daily, or **Recharge 16+** for a flame path devotee
Target: 1d3 nearby enemies in a group; *breath weapon*
Breath Weapon: For the rest of the battle, roll a d20 at the start of each of your turns; on a 16+, you can use *flame breath* that turn if you wish.
Attack: Charisma + Level vs. PD
Hit: 3d6 + Charisma fire damage.
Miss: Half damage.

3rd level spell	5d6 damage
5th level spell	4d10 damage
7th level spell	6d12 damage
9th level spell	10d12 damage

Adventurer Feat: If you have a positive or conflicted relationship with the Great Gold Wyrm, natural even *flame breath* attack rolls against demons deal maximum damage.
Champion Feat: If you have a positive or conflicted relationship with the Great Gold Wyrm, you gain a +1 bonus to *flame breath* re-use rolls during the battle and flame breath recharge rolls after the battle.
Epic Feat: If you have a positive or conflicted relationship with the Great Gold Wyrm, you gain flight during any turn you use *flame breath*. The flight lasts until the end of your next turn.

FLICKERING

Twice per day, before rolling initiative, you can decide to use flickering power in an upcoming battle.

If your natural initiative roll in a battle is odd, you take a –1 penalty to all defenses. If your natural initiative roll is even, you gain a +2 bonus to all defenses.

Each time you are hit by an attack, your situation flips after the **Attack:** the –1 penalty becomes a +2 bonus, or the +2 bonus becomes a –1 penalty.

Adventurer Feat: Once per battle you can choose not to flip the bonus/penalty.

Champion Feat: The defense penalty is now –2. The defense bonus is now +4.

DANCE IN FLAMES

Once per battle when an enemy moves to engage you, you can roll a normal save (11+) as an interrupt action. If the save succeeds, deal 5 ongoing fire damage to that enemy (5th level: 10 ongoing fire damage; 8th level: 15 ongoing fire damage).

Adventurer Feat: You can use the Dance in Flames save twice per battle.

Champion Feat: If you are a flame path devotee, you can use the Dance in Flames save at-will, though it still requires an interrupt action (and is therefore likely to apply only once per round).

Epic Feat: Once per battle, you can use Dance in Flames as a free action.

FLARE-UP

You can use this power a number of times each day equal to your Constitution modifier.

As a free action when an enemy saves with a natural odd roll against an effect you caused with a demonologist spell or power, move the spell effect off the creature that just saved to a nearby enemy.

As for the corruption path Contagion power, Flare Up can't move an effect created by one of your summoned creatures.

Adventurer Feat: Once per battle, if you are conscious when the escalation die reaches 5+, gain another use of the Flare Up power that day.

Champion Feat: You can now use the power even if the target fails the save. As before, the effect moves off the target onto a new creature of your choice.

Epic Feat: Saves against spell effects and ongoing damage you have moved using this talent are 2 points harder. (Easy: 8+, etc.)

MASTER OF FLAMES

You gain the wizard cantrips *light* and *spark* (*13th Age* core rulebook, page 147), and can cast them at-will as a quick action.

When you choose spells during a full heal-up, you can replace one demonologist flame path spell you would choose with another spell that does fire damage from a different class. You cast this spell at your demonologist level, replacing the ability score for attack and damage with Charisma, and any other ability score mentioned with Constitution.

Adventurer Feat: You gain the adventurer feat, if any, for the spell you choose from a different class.

Champion Feat: Ditto for the champion feat.

Epic Feat: And for the epic feat.

FLAME BONUS SPELL

Flame **initiates** gain *summon flame demon* as a daily spell.

Flame path **devotees** have *summon flame demon* as a recharge 16+ spell.

Flame path **fanatics** instead have the spell as a recharge 11+ spell.

SUMMON FLAME DEMON

Ranged Spell

Usage depends on talents in path

Effect: You summon a demon to fight for you until the end of the battle as a superior (but degrading!) summoned creature. The demon summoned is determined by the level you cast the spell at, as follows:

1st level spell	summon burner
3rd level spell	summon hellhound
5th level spell	summon fire-imp
7th level spell	summon glabrezu
9th level spell	summon balor

FLAME PATH LEVEL PROGRESSION

Demonologist Level	Flame Initiate Spells	Flame Devotee Spells	Flame Fanatic Spells	Spell Level
Level 1 Multiclass	*1*	*1*	2	*1st level*
Level 1	1	2	3	1st level
Level 2	1	3	4	1st level
Level 3	2	3	4	3rd level
Level 4	2	4	5	3rd level
Level 5	2	5	6	5th level
Level 6	3	5	6	5th level
Level 7	3	6	7	7th level
Level 8	3	6	7	7th level
Level 9	3	7	8	9th level
Level 10	3	7	8	9th level

SUMMONED BURNER

1st level archer [DEMON]
Initiative: +7

Flickers of flame +7 vs. AC—3 fire damage

R: Flickers of flame +7 vs. AC—5 fire damage
Miss: Deal 3 fire damage to a random nearby creature (yes, could be enemy or ally!).

Quick flicking fire: The summoned burner adds escalation die to its disengage checks.

Flight: Bobs along low to the ground, if it gets higher than 6' it drops, as if tethered to the earth.

Degradation: At the end of each of its turns, the summoned burner suffers 1d6 damage.

AC	17	
PD	15	**HP 24 (Initiate: 20)**
MD	13	

SUMMONED HELLHOUND

3rd level wrecker [DEMON]
Initiative: +5

Savage bite +9 vs. AC—6 damage
Natural even hit or miss: The hellhound can make a *fiery breath attack* as a free action.

[Special trigger] **C: Fiery breath +9 vs. PD (1d3 nearby enemies in a group)**—8 fire damage

Resist fire 16+: When a fire attack targets this creature, the attacker must roll a natural 16+ on the attack roll or it only deals half damage.

Degradation: At the end of each of its turns, the summoned hellhound suffers 3d6 damage.

AC	17	
PD	15	**HP 58 (Initiate: 48)**
MD	11	

Summoned Big Burner

5th level archer [DEMON]
Initiative: +11

Flickers of flame +11 vs. AC—10 fire damage

R: Flickers of flame +11 vs. AC—18 fire damage
Miss: Deal 10 fire damage to a random nearby creature (yes, could be enemy or ally!).

Quick flicking fire: Adds the escalation die to its disengage checks.

Flight: Bobs along low to the ground, if it gets higher than 6' it drops, as if tethered to the earth.

Degradation: At the end of each of its turns, the summoned big burner suffers 3d6 damage.

AC	21	
PD	19	**HP 66** (Initiate: 56)
MD	17	

Summoned Pincer Demon

7th level caster [DEMON]
Initiative: +14

Pincer +12 vs. AC—20 fire damage
Natural even hit: 10 ongoing damage

R: Painbolt +12 vs. MD (one nearby or far away creature)—35 psychic damage

C: Hellfire + 12 vs. PD (1d3 nearby enemies in a group and any glabrezou allies engaged with those enemies)—25 fire damage

Degradation: At the end of each of its turns, the summoned pincer demon suffers 4d12 damage.

AC	20	
PD	20	**HP 170** (Initiate: 144)
MD	16	

Summoned Lesser Balor

Large 9th level wrecker [DEMON]
Initiative: +13

Abyssal blade +14 vs. AC—50 damage
Natural even hit: The balor deals +1d8 lightning damage to the target and to one other nearby enemy of balor's choice. Then repeat that damage roll against the targets once for each point on the escalation die (so if it's 4, that's four more d8 rolls)
Natural even miss: 25 damage.

C: Flaming whip +14 vs. PD (one nearby enemy)—15 fire damage, and the target is pulled to the balor, who engages it.
Natural even miss: 7 fire damage.
Limited use: 1/round, as a quick action.

Desperate escalator: While staggered, the balor adds the escalation die to its attack rolls.

Flight: Giant bat wings are good for something besides looking tough.

Shadow and flame: When out of control, but not before, the summoned lesser balor gains a +5 bonus to all defenses against attacks by far away enemies.

Degradation: At the end of each of its turns, the summoned lesser balor suffers 1d10 x 10 damage.

AC	24	
PD	22	**HP 340** (Initiate: 290)
MD	18	

FLAME SPELLS

1st LEVEL FLAME SPELLS

BURN IT OFF

Ranged spell

Special: You take half-damage on the second and subsequent castings of this spell in a battle.

Once per battle, or **at-will for flame path devotee** (but see special!)

Target: Nearby enemy

Attack: Charisma + Level vs. PD

Hit: 2d6 + Charisma fire damage.

Natural even hit: Subtract 2 from the target's AC until the end of the battle (not cumulative).

Miss: —

3rd level spell	4d6 damage
5th level spell	6d6 damage
7th level spell	9d6 damage
9th level spell	8d12 damage

Adventurer Feat: Burn it off now deals miss damage equal to your level.

Champion Feat: Spell is now cumulative up to −4 AC.

Epic Feat: The penalty now also applies to PD.

FEED THE FLAME DEMONS

Ranged spell

At-Will

Special: You can't cast the spell while a creature is taking ongoing fire damage from a previous casting of the spell.

Target: One nearby enemy

Attack: Charisma + Level vs. PD

Hit: 2d8 + Charisma modifier fire damage, and 5 ongoing fire damage.

Miss: Deal 5 ongoing fire damage to a random nearby ally.

3rd level spell	4d8 damage and 10 ongoing damage
5th level spell	6d8 damage and 15 ongoing damage
7th level spell	8d8 damage and 20 ongoing damage
9th level spell	12d8 damage and 30 ongoing damage

EVERBURN

Ranged spell

Recharge 16+ after battle

Target: One nearby enemy

Attack: Charisma + Level vs. PD

Hit: 1d8 + Charisma fire damage, and the target takes 5 ongoing fire damage and is vulnerable (hard save ends both, 16+).

Miss: Half damage, and the target takes 5 ongoing fire damage and is vulnerable (save ends both).

3rd level spell	3d8 damage, 15 ongoing damage and in addition to being vulnerable, the target can't turn invisible or hide from you or your allies (save ends all)
5th level spell	5d8 damage, 25 ongoing damage and the target also can't teleport (save ends all)
7th level spell	7d8 damage and 35 ongoing damage
9th level spell	10d8 damage and 50 ongoing damage

FLAME SHROUD

Close-quarters spell

At-Will

Target: 1 enemy you are engaged with

Attack: Charisma + Level vs. PD

Natural even hit: 9 damage, and you can pop free of target.

Natural odd hit: 7 damage

Miss: Damage equal to your level, and you cannot target this enemy with *flame shroud* again this battle.

3rd level spell	Even 16 damage, odd 11 damage
5th level spell	Even 25 damage, odd 19 damage
7th level spell	Even 36 damage, odd 28 damage
9th level spell	Even 62 damage, odd 47 damage

WHIPPING TONGUES OF FIRE

Close-quarters curse spell

Recharge 16+ after battle

Quick action to cast

Curse Effect: As an interrupt action later in the battle, or as a free action if you've already spent your interrupt action this round *on this curse*, deal 10 ongoing fire damage to a nearby enemy that attacks with a natural odd attack roll; the curse effect can be used a number of times this battle equal to your Constitution modifier.

3rd level spell	15 ongoing fire damage
5th level spell	20 ongoing fire damage
7th level spell	35 ongoing fire damage
9th level spell	50 ongoing fire damage

3ᴿᴰ LEVEL FLAME SPELLS

KEEP BURNING PLEASE

Close-quarters spell

Recharge 11+ after battle

Interrupt action

Target: A nearby enemy that just saved against ongoing fire damage

Attack: Charisma + Level vs PD.

Hit: The target fails the saving throw instead, and increase the ongoing fire damage by 2d6.

Miss: Regain the use of this spell.

5ᵗʰ level spell	Damage increases by 4d6
7ᵗʰ level spell	Damage increases by 3d12
9ᵗʰ level spell	Damage increases by 5d12

Adventurer Feat: Spell is now recharge 6+.

Champion Feat: If you keep the enemy burning, the save against the ongoing damage is now a hard save (16+), if it wasn't already.

Epic Feat: When you keep the enemy burning, it takes the new amount of ongoing fire damage immediately.

FLAMING TELEPORT

Close-quarters spell

Move action to cast

Recharge 6+ after battle

Target: One nearby creature taking ongoing fire damage

Effect: Teleport next to that creature. You can choose whether to be engaged with that creature (or next to them if they're an ally) or extremely close to the creature but not engaged.

5ᵗʰ level spell	*Flaming teleport* now only requires a quick action to cast
7ᵗʰ level spell	Target can now be far away
9ᵗʰ level spell	*Flaming teleport* can now also be used to teleport away from engagement with an enemy that is taking ongoing fire damage

Adventurer Feat: If you are a flame path devotee, deal the ongoing fire damage the target is taking to the target if you teleport into engagement with it.

Champion Feat: Spell is now once per battle instead of recharge 6+.

Epic Feat: If a creature is reduced to 0 hit points by ongoing fire damage, you can *flaming teleport* to teleport to their former location on your next turn, even if the spell has been expended. (Yes, this would also let you teleport next to an ally dropped by ongoing fire damage!)

INCOMPATIBLE BURNS

The Flare Up talent and *keep burning please* fit the same theme, but they can't actually both be used at the same time. Using the interrupt action to cast *keep burning please* prevents the save from having succeeded, the precondition for using Flare Up. It still works well to have both options . . .

SWARMING FLAME DEMONS

Close-quarters spell

Recharge 11+ after battle

Target: 1d3 nearby enemies

Attack: Charisma + Level vs. PD

Hit: 20 fire damage.

Miss: Damage equal to twice your level

Effect: Regardless of your attack rolls, the next time an enemy rolls a natural 1-5 with an attack this battle, deal 3d6 fire damage to that creature and each enemy nearby them as the flame demons swarm (only deal this damage once to each mob of mooks).

5ᵗʰ level spell	30 fire damage on a hit, 5d6 effect damage
7ᵗʰ level spell	50 fire damage on a hit, 8d6 effect damage
9ᵗʰ level spell	80 fire damage on a hit, 8d10 effect damage

5ᵀᴴ LEVEL FLAME SPELLS

GOLDEN CLAW

Close-quarters spell

Daily

Effect: You conjure a great flaming claw that you can ride around the battle. You gain flight, but cannot fly above head height. You also gain a +2 bonus to all defenses. When you would be hit by a melee attack, you can choose to respond with the claw's attack as an interrupt action, possibly canceling the attack if you eliminate the attacker (and/or losing the claw, as you'll see below!). The claw lasts until the end of the battle, or until you've lost it.

The Golden Claw's Attack

Target: Enemy that hit you with an attack

Attack: Charisma + Level vs. AC

Hit: 6d10 damage

Natural 19-20: 15 ongoing fire damage to the target OR a different nearby enemy, and the *golden claw* spell ends, taking you to the ground before disappearing.

Miss: 5 damage.

7th level spell	10d10 claw damage, 7 miss damage
9th level spell	3d4 x 10 claw damage, 9 miss damage

Champion Feat: If you have at least one relationship point with the Great Gold Wyrm, you can use the *golden claw's attack* as a quick action 1d3 times each battle you cast the spell. 1/round only!

Epic Feat: If you are a flame path devotee, *golden claw* is now a recharge 16+ spell.

KINDLING

Ranged Spell

Recharge 16+

Special: If the target is engaged with one of your summoned demons double the ongoing damage if you hit.

Target: One nearby enemy

Attack: Charisma + Level vs PD

Hit: 6d10 + Charisma fire damage, and 15 ongoing fire damage; while the target is taking this ongoing fire damage, your allies and summoned creatures have a +2 attack bonus against the target.

Miss: Half damage.

7th level spell	9d10 damage, and 20 ongoing fire damage
9th level spell	3d10 x 10 damage, and 40 ongoing fire damage

Champion Feat: Can now be used against a far away target, and add 10 to ongoing damage.

Epic Feat: Attack bonus for allies and summoned creatures increases to +4.

7TH LEVEL FLAME SPELL

PYRES

Ranged spell

Daily

Target: 1d3 + 1 nearby enemies

Attack: Charisma + Level vs. PD

Hit: 8d10 + Charisma modifier fire damage, and 25 ongoing fire damage. Increase this ongoing damage by 1d10 each time a non-mook enemy or the last mook in a mob drops to 0 hit points!

Miss: 25 ongoing fire damage.

9th level spell	2d8 x 10 fire damage, 40 ongoing fire damage, and increase by 2d10 each time an enemy drops to 0 hit points

Champion Feat: Increase the number of targets to 1d4 + 2.

Epic Feat: On any turn a target does not move, the save against ongoing damage becomes a hard save.

9TH LEVEL FLAME SPELL

GOROGAN'S BREATH

Close-quarters spell

Daily

Special: This spell cannot be used in the overworld. Also see the spell effect for its repeated impact on the battle.

Target: 1d8 nearby non-flying enemies. Each enemy can only be targeted once.

Attack: Charisma + Level vs. PD

Hit: 10d6 + Charisma fire damage.

Miss: Half damage. Allies (including you) engaged with the target you missed take one-quarter damage.

Effect: You can repeat the attack 1/round as a quick action on your next turn, and on each of your subsequent turns this battle, until you fail to use the attack on your turn. Each use of the spell after the first deals damage to you equal to 1d12 for each time you have used this spell after the first.

Epic Feat: Increase the damage to 10d10 + Charisma fire damage.

SLAUGHTER PATH

Slaughter path devotees are committed to the idea that if you're going to summon demons, it helps to be wearing heavy armor and swinging a big sword.

ARMORED DESTROYER

As a slaughter path **initiate** or **devotee**, your AC in light armor is 13.

As a slaughter path **initiate**, your AC in heavy armor is 14, with a −2 attack penalty.

If you are a slaughter path **devotee**, you lose the attack penalty for wearing heavy armor and using shields.

DEMONIC WARRIOR

This feature only applies to slaughter path devotees. Initiates get nothing out of this.

You lose the attack penalty for using heavy or martial melee weapons: you're happy swinging warhammers, flails, swords, and other nasty and spiky serious weapons.

In addition, your basic melee attacks deal damage equal to your level on a miss.

In addition, and perhaps most significantly, your basic melee attacks use your Charisma as their attack and damage ability score while you are not staggered.

When you are staggered, your basic melee attacks revert to using your Strength, as normal.

(See the Ravager talent below for another melee ability connected to not being staggered.)

> **Adventurer Feat:** One turn per battle when you are staggered, use your Charisma as your attack and damage ability score with basic melee attacks instead of your Strength.
>
> **Champion Feat:** Once per day, as a free action, you do not count as staggered until the end of the battle, unless you are at 0 hit points.

RESIST MELEE DAMAGE

Slaughter path **initiates** gain *resist melee damage 10+*, taking half damage from melee attacks unless the attack's natural attack roll is 10+.

For slaughter path **devotees**, the power increases to *resist melee damage 12+*.

For slaughter path **fanatics**, the power increases to *resist melee damage 14+*.

> **Adventurer Feat:** Your recovery dice are d8s instead of d6s.
>
> **Champion Feat:** If you are a slaughter path devotee, your base hit points increase from 6 to 7.
>
> **Epic Feat:** Your recovery dice are d10s instead of d8s.

BONUS SUMMONING SPELL

Slaughter **initiates** gain *summon slaughter demon* as a daily spell. (The spell appears on page 28.)

Slaughter path **devotees** instead have *summon slaughter demon* as a recharge 16+ spell.

Slaughter path **fanatics** have *summon slaughter demon* as a recharge 11+ spell.

SLAUGHTER PATH TALENTS

BLOOD & SLAUGHTER

You have a bonus daily use of the *summon slaughter demon* spell at your normal highest level.

This bonus casting of the spell functions exactly like your usual casting of the spell, but with the following complication: when the demon summoned by the spell is hit by an attack with a natural odd attack roll, you take damage equal to half the damage that the summoned demon takes. No *resist damage* ability from demonologist paths or any other source reduces this damage.

DEMONIC VIOLENCE

Use this power a number of times each day equal to your Constitution modifier + 1.

When you move to engage an enemy you were not engaged with at the start of your turn, deal 1d6 damage to that enemy as you engage them.

This power improves as you gain levels.

2nd level demonologist	2d4 damage
3rd level demonologist	2d6 damage
4th level demonologist	2d8 damage
5th level demonologist	3d6 damage
6th level demonologist	3d8 damage
7th level demonologist	4d8 damage
8th level demonologist	5d8 damage
9th level demonologist	5d10 damage
10th level demonologist	5d12 damage

> **Adventurer Feat:** If you have a positive or conflicted relationship with the Crusader, gain an additional 1d3 uses of this power each day. (Yes, roll at the start of the day.).
>
> **Champion Feat:** Add double your Charisma modifier to the damage dealt with Focused Violence (8th level: triple your Charisma modifier).
>
> **Epic Feat:** If you eliminate a non-mook enemy using this power, you gain an extra standard action this turn.

BLOOD & SLAUGHTER MATH

Note that you're not taking the damage instead of the demon—your demon takes the damage normally, then you take half that damage. On average, you'll take ¼ of the damage that enemies deal to the demon you'll summon using this bonus spell. You don't take anything from the degradation damage, and you stop taking damage from the complication if the demon drops to 0 hit points and goes out of your control.

DEMONIC REINFORCEMENTS

Once per day when one of your demonologist attacks drops a non-mook enemy to 0 hit points, roll a save. The type of save depends on the size and level of the creature.

If the creature is a normal creature, the save starts as an easy save (6+). If the creature is a large or double-strength creature, it's a normal save (11+). If you're higher level than the target, add the difference in levels to the save as a bonus. If you are lower level than the target, subtract the difference in levels as a penalty.

The power doesn't work against a huge or triple-strength creature.

If the save succeeds, the enemy does not drop to 0 hit points. Instead, set its hit points equal to half its staggered value and give the creature the *degradation* ability that appears below. Until the end of the battle, or until it is destroyed, the creature fights for you as if it were confused (in other words, using its at-will attacks). Unlike the demons you summon that take degradation damage, this creature merely dies when it again reaches 0 hit points, you don't have to save to see if it goes out of control, it was your enemy once already.

Degradation: At the end of each of its turns, the Demonic Reinforcements creature suffers 3 x its level damage (large or double-strength: 6 x level, huge or triple-strength: 9 x level).

Adventurer Feat: Once per day, when your Demonic Reinforcements save fails, you do not expend the ability.

Champion Feat: You can now target a huge or triple-strength creature with Demonic Reinforcements, but the save is a hard save (16+).

Epic Feat: You gain a +2 bonus to saves made to use this talent.

PLAYERS

The creature you create using Demonic Reinforcements isn't the same creature you've been fighting—it's a disembodied demon taking over the dead creature's body. That qualifies as some type of demonic necromancy unless you fight for the Crusader, in which case it's efficient use of controllable resources.

RAVAGER

While you are not staggered, you deal half damage with your basic melee attacks that miss.

Adventurer Feat: If you are a slaughter path devotee, two battles per day you can use the Ravager power to deal half damage with basic melee attacks that miss even when you are staggered.

Champion Feat: If you are a slaughter path devotee, you can reroll a basic melee attack that misses a number of times each day equal to your Charisma modifier.

Epic Feat: Once per battle you can reroll the damage of one of your melee attacks.

SACRIFICIAL BLADE

Once per battle when your attack drops a non-mook* to 0 hit points, or you eliminate the last mook in a mob, roll a normal save (11+). If the save succeeds, you can take a free standard action this turn. (*The exception is that slaying your summoned creature, or any creature summoned by an ally, does not trigger sacrificial blade.)

Adventurer Feat: The save is now an easy save (6+) instead of a normal save.

Champion Feat: You can use the ability twice each battle instead of once, though only once per turn.

Epic Feat: You can also attempt to use Sacrificial Blade if one of your summoned demons strikes the killing blow.

SLAUGHTER BONUS SPELL

Slaughter **initiates** gain *summon slaughter demon* as a bonus daily spell.

Slaughter path **devotees** instead have *summon slaughter demon* as a bonus recharge 16+ spell.

Slaughter path **fanatics** instead have *summon slaughter demon* as a recharge 11+ spell.

SUMMON SLAUGHTER DEMON

Ranged Spell

Usage varies based on slaughter path talents

Effect: You summon a demon to fight for you until the end of the battle as a superior (but degrading!) summoned creature. The demon summoned is determined by the level you cast the spell at, as follows:

1st level spell	summon claw demon
3rd level spell	summon hungry maw
5th level spell	summon frenzy demon
7th level spell	summon laughing demon
9th level spell	summon marilith

SUMMONED CLAW DEMON

1st level troop [DEMON]
Initiative: +6

Hooking claws +6 vs. AC (1d3 attacks)—3 damage

Degradation: At the end of each of its turns, the summoned claw demon suffers 1d6 damage.

AC	**17**	
PD	14	**HP 24** (Initiate: 20)
MD	11	

SUMMONED HUNGRY MAW

3rd level blocker [DEMON]
Initiative: +6

Big chomp +9 vs. AC—12 damage
  Natural even hit: Target and hungry maw are both stuck until the end of the hungry maw's next turn, or until they are not engaged with each other.

Chomp and chew: If the hungry maw starts its turns stuck and engaged with a stuck enemy, it loses its standard action this turn but automatically deals 8 damage and 4 ongoing damage to that enemy.

Degradation: At the end of each of its turns, the summoned hungry maw suffers 2d6 damage.

AC	**16**	
PD	16	**HP 48** (Initiate: 40)
MD	12	

SLAUGHTER PATH LEVEL PROGRESSION

Demonologist Level	Slaughter Initiate Spells	Slaughter Devotee Spells	Slaughter Fanatic Spells	Spell Level
Level 1 Multiclass	*1*	*1*	*2*	*1st level*
Level 1	1	2	3	1st level
Level 2	1	3	4	1st level
Level 3	1	3	4	3rd level
Level 4	1	4	5	3rd level
Level 5	2	4	5	5th level
Level 6	2	4	5	5th level
Level 7	2	5	6	7th level
Level 8	2	5	6	7th level
Level 9	2	5	6	9th level
Level 10	3	6	7	9th level

SUMMONED FRENZY DEMON

5th level wrecker [DEMON]
Initiative: +10

Claw +8 vs. AC (2 attacks)—7 damage

Raging frenzy: Whenever the frenzy demon misses with a melee attack, it gains a +1 attack bonus and deals +1d4 damage until the end of the battle (maximum bonus +4, +4d4).

Degradation: At the end of each of its turns, the summoned frenzy demon suffers 4d6 damage.

AC	20	
PD	16	**HP 70** (Initiate: 56)
MD	16	

SUMMONED LAUGHING DEMON

7th level troop [DEMON]
Initiative: +11

Tooth & claw and stomp +12 vs. AC—22 damage
Miss: 11 damage

Won't ... stop... laughing: While one or more summoned laughing demons are in a battle deal 8 psychic damage to each enemy who fails a save.

Degradation: At the end of each of its turns, the summoned laughing demon suffers 6d6 damage.

AC	22	
PD	17	**HP 124** (Initiate: 100)
MD	19	

SUMMONED MARILITH

Large 9th level troop [DEMON]
Initiative: +17

Three whirling swords +14 vs. AC (3 attacks)—18 damage, and the marilith can pop free from the target after the attacks

R: Beguiling gaze +14 vs. MD (one nearby or far away unengaged enemy)—As a free action, the target immediately moves toward the marilith, attempting to engage it or get as close as possible to it
Limited use: 1/round, as a quick action.

Terrible swift swords: When the escalation die is even, the summoned marilith's crit range with melee attacks expands by a number equal to the escalation die. If the summoned marilith is out of control, its crit range expands by a number equal to the escalation die whether the die is even or odd.

Degradation: At the end of each of its turns, the summoned marilith suffers 10d6 damage.

AC	24	
PD	17	**HP 200** (Initiate: 165)
MD	21	

1ST LEVEL SLAUGHTER SPELLS

BLADE POLISHED IN BLOOD
Close-quarters spell
Once per battle
Quick action to cast
Special: You must have reduced a non-mook creature (or the last mook of a mob) to zero hit points with a basic or at-will melee attack this turn.
Effect: You can spend a recovery.
Adventurer Feat: If you are a slaughter path devotee, add your Charisma modifier to the healing from the recovery (5th level: double your Charisma modifier; 8th level: triple).
Champion Feat: If you are a slaughter path devotee, you can cast this spell twice per battle, though only once a turn.
Epic Feat: If you are still staggered after using the recovery, the recovery is free.

Hate

Close-quarters spell

Once per battle

Quick action to cast

Target: Yourself

Effect: The first time you hit with a weapon attack this turn, add 5 to the damage.

3rd level spell	8
5th level spell	13
7th level spell	20
9th level spell	33

Adventurer Feat: You can now cast *hate* twice per battle.

Champion Feat: The bonus damage now also applies if your first attack misses this turn.

Epic Feat: Once per day, *hate* applies to every attack you make this turn, not just the first.

Reckless Slaughter

Close spell

Recharge 11+ after battle

Quick action to cast

Effect: Make a basic melee attack using the ability score of your choice as the attack and damage stat and using d12s for the damage die. On a miss, you inflict no damage on the target and instead hit an ally engaged with the target for one-quarter damage. If no allies are engaged, hit an ally next to you and if no allies are next to you, hit yourself instead.

3rd level spell	Add 7 to the damage if the attack hits
5th level spell	Add 13 to the damage if the attack hits
7th level spell	Add 20 to the damage if the attack hits
9th level spell	Add 25 to the damage if the attack hits

Adventurer Feat: If you are a slaughter path devotee, *reckless slaughter* is now a recharge 6+ spell.

The Rending

Close-quarters spell

Recharge 16+ after battle

Target: 1 nearby or far away enemy

Attack: Charisma + Level vs. PD

Hit: 3d12 + Charisma damage

Miss: Half damage, and you OR an ally engaged with the target also take half *that* damage.

3rd level spell	5d12 damage
5th level spell	8d12 damage
7th level spell	2d8 x 10 damage
9th level spell	4d6 x 10 damage

Adventurer Feat: If you miss all targets (see champion feat!) with *the rending*, it's a recharge 6+ spell after the battle.

Champion Feat: Once per day, when the escalation die is 2+, *the rending* can target two enemies instead of one. (Obviously if it misses twice, you or allies are taking a good deal of damage.)

3rd Level Slaughter Spells

Death Mark

Close-quarters spell

Daily, OR **Recharge 16+** after battle, for a slaughter path devotee

Quick action to cast

Effect: Your summoned creatures gain a +3 attack bonus until the end of the battle against any creature you hit with an attack this battle. (This applies even if you summon the creature after the attack.)

Adventurer Feat: In addition, add your Charisma modifier to the damage dealt by hits from your summoned creatures' attacks against enemies you hit yourself (5th level: double your Charisma modifier; 8th level: triple your Charisma modifier).

Champion Feat: In addition, any creature you hit with an attack this battle is vulnerable to the attacks of your summoned creatures.

Deceptive Wound

Close-quarters spell

Recharge 11+ after battle

Quick action to cast

Target: Creature you hit with a melee attack earlier this turn.

Effect: Deal 10 ongoing damage to the target, easy save (6+) ends. The first time the target fails the save, the save becomes a normal save (11+). If the target fails that save also, the save becomes a hard save (16+).

5th level spell	15 ongoing damage
7th level spell	25 ongoing damage
9th level spell	40 ongoing damage

Follow the Blood

Close-quarters spell

Cast as an interrupt action

Recharge 11+ after battle, or **once per battle** for slaughter devotee

Target: One nearby enemy that becomes staggered, but still has hit points greater than 0.

Effect: Teleport into engagement with the target.

5th level spell	Spell can now also target an enemy that has been reduced to 0 hit points OR an ally that has been staggered or reduced to 0 hit points
7th level spell	If the spell targets a staggered enemy, that enemy is vulnerable to your attacks until the end of the battle (your slaughter path talents might also deal damage to it automatically)
9th level spell	Now a recharge 6+ spell

Epic Feat: You can use this spell when you become staggered to teleport next to a nearby staggered creature.

Implacable Destruction

Close-quarters spell

Recharge 16+ after battle, or **Recharge 11+** for a slaughter path devotee

Special: So long as you are conscious, this spell ignores any effect you are under that would prevent or hinder you from casting the spell and making its associated attack (being confused or stunned, attack penalties from being dazed or weakened, etc.).

Effect: Make a basic or at-will attack with a +2 bonus.

> *Adventurer Feat:* Recharge becomes 11+, or 6+ for a devotee.
>
> *Champion Feat:* On a hit, one effect that was suspended by the spell ends, provided the GM can see how that makes any sense.
>
> *Epic Feat:* You do not expend this spell if the attack misses.

5TH LEVEL SLAUGHTER SPELLS

Altar Reversal

Close-quarters spell

Recharge 16+ after battle, or **recharge 11+** for a slaughter path devotee

Quick action to cast

Effect: Until the end of the turn, you gain a +4 attack bonus against demons, and demons are vulnerable to your attacks. If you use this opportunity to attack a 5th or lower level slaughter demon you summoned that is still under your control, and drop the demon's hit points to 0 with the attack, you automatically succeed with the save that determines whether you lose control of the demon. Instead you roll a normal save (11+) to see if you regain the use of your summoning spell! (**GM:** This is the right time to enforce the rule that a summoned demon takes its turn after its summoner's turn. The demonologist should be attempting to cut its demon down before the demon can attack that round.)

7th level spell	Now affects any of your 7th level summoned demons
9th level spell	Now affects your 9th level summoned demons, and your critical hits against demons deal triple damage until the end of the battle

Champion Feat: Instead of you, one nearby ally gains the attack bonus and vulnerability effect against demons.

Epic Feat: Both you and one nearby ally gain the attack bonus and vulnerability effect.

Mass Slaughter

Close-quarters spell

Daily

Effect: Make a separate basic melee attack against each of 1d3+1 enemies engaged with you. For each hit, also deal half the damage to a different nearby random creature you are not engaged with. Each creature can only be damaged once with the attacks/spell.

7th level spell	You can exclude one nearby ally from being a possible random target of the secondary damage
9th level spell	You can now exclude two nearby allies from being a possible random target of the secondary damage

Champion Feat: If you miss all targets with this spell, regain it after a quick rest.

Epic Feat: Your attacks with this spell deal half damage on a miss.

7TH LEVEL SLAUGHTER SPELL

Death is Everywhere

Close Spell

Recharge 16+

Effect: Teleport someplace nearby and make a basic or at-will attack against a single target. If that attack hits, repeat the effect against an enemy you have not already attacked with *death is everywhere* this turn. So long as you keep hitting, you can continue teleporting and attacking until you have made a number of attacks with the spell equal to your Constitution modifier.

Champion Feat: If your first attack misses, regain this spell after a quick rest.

Epic Feat: If you roll an even miss with an attack made from this spell, repeat the effect.

9TH LEVEL SLAUGHTER SPELL

Blood for Blood!

Close-quarters spell

Daily

Effect: Deal 1d20 damage to yourself. Then attack and automatically critically hit one enemy with a basic melee weapon attack as if you had rolled a natural 20.

Epic Feat: Your critical hit deals triple damage.

DEMONOLOGIST MULTICLASS

If you're interested in multiclassing rules, you either already own *13 True Ways* or you're about to go pick up a copy! Use the multiclassing rules that start on page 103 of *13TW* in conjunction with the new key modifier table and demonologist multiclassing notes below.

Design note: We haven't played any multiclass demonologists. Many demonologists mix paths, and that may already feel a bit like playing a multiclass character. That could discourage players from *needing* to multiclass or it may encourage further experimentation, we can see it working both ways.

Since all three talents are required to be a fanatic of one the demonologist paths, there are no fanatic multiclass demonologists. Fanatics don't yield a talent to be given to another class.

Level progression: You lag one level behind in the powers and spells known columns of the three path-specific demonologist level progression tables. The tables contain a multiclass entry that shows what you'll get as 1st level multiclass demonologist on each of the paths.

Control issues: As a multiclass demonologist, it's a tiny bit harder to stay in control of your summoned demons when they drop to 0 hit points. For most demonologists, the control save is an easy save, 6+. For you it's a 7+ save. It's really not that big a deal, more a token of your distraction.

Forking paths: Multiclassing highlights the two distinct styles of demonologists, the spellcasters who prefer to stay back (corruption, flame) and the armored warriors who are comfortable near the front line (slaughter). As you'll see in the key modifier table, we've separated the two styles, they have different ability score conditions.

Skillful warriors: In fact, slaughter path devotees count as skillful warriors who do not suffer the weapon damage penalty from multiclassing so long as their multiclass combo includes another skillful warrior. The full list: barbarian, bard, commander, slaughter path demonologist devotee, fighter, paladin, ranger, rogue. See page 105 of *13TW* for the standard rule.

In addition, if it fits the story for the multiclass demonologist in your campaign, feel free to let them choose the Armored Warfare feats listed for the fighter multiclass on page 109 of *13TW*.

The intelligent tiefling: For simplicity's sake, we're going to treat the demonologist class feature named That's Intelligent (page 9) as if it was a talent, so that's it's not an exception to the key feature modifier rules on page 106 of *13TW*. There's no reason to let multiclass tiefling demonologists get around the key modifier rules that other multiclass characters have to cope with.

DEMONOLOGIST MULTICLASS KEY MODIFIER TABLE

Multiclass	Corruption and Flame Path Initiates or Devotees	Slaughter Path Devotees
Barbarian	Str/Cha	*Str/Cha*
Bard	Str OR Dex/Cha	*Str/Cha*
Chaos mage	Int/Cha	Str/Cha
Cleric	Wis/Cha	Wis/Cha
Commander	Str/Cha	*Str/Cha*
Druid	Wis/Cha	Str/Cha
Fighter	Str/Cha	*Str/Cha*
Monk	Dex/Cha	Dex/Cha
Necromancer	Int/Cha	Int/Cha
Occultist	Int/Cha	Int/Cha
Paladin	Str/Cha	*Str/Cha*
Ranger	Str OR Dex/Cha	*Str/Cha*
Rogue	Dex/Cha	*Dex/Cha*
Sorcerer	Con/Cha	Con/Cha
Wizard	Int/Cha	Int/Cha

CHAPTER 2

GAMEMASTERING DEMONS

Demons! Demons! Demons!

They're the worst of creatures and the best of villains. This chapter is a bit of a grab bag for the folks behind the GM screen. Sections include:

- A look at some of the reasons demons make such great villains.
- Ideas for making demons more distinctive in your campaign.
- Demonic arguments to appeal to followers of all 13 icons, especially those who should know better!
- The ecology of the hellhole.
- Monster stats for the new demons introduced in the demonologist, and new random demon abilities.

SALUTING THE WORST

Before we talk about how to get the most out of demons in your game, let's salute the virtues of these most unvirtuous foes.

EVERYBODY HATES DEMONS

Demons want to destroy the world. That puts them at odds with everyone who lives in the world—which is everyone. Every other major monster type has an arguable degree of ambiguity. Undead have angst, and the Lich King has come to the defense of the Empire in the past. The Orc Lord, if not all orcs, has some potential justification for his thirst for vengeance and conquest.

But everyone, even the Diabolist, beats up demons with a clear conscience. If you need a monster type that every icon relationship, character class, background or character concept is always willing to kill, go for demons. Even demons are happy to kill demons—there's no loyalty in hell.

THREE ICONS ARE DEMON-OBSESSED

If you imagine a Venn diagram of spheres of interest and influence among the icons, then demons figure prominently on it, up there with magic and the fate of the Empire as primary concerns. Demons threaten everyone, but three Icons—the Crusader, the Diabolist, and the Great Gold Wyrm—are especially concerned

with demons. As you'll have read above, we think of the new demonologist class as a product of this three-way demonic entanglement.

DEMONS HATE YOU

Demons are naturally malicious and cruel. They are inherently evil, existing purely to sow chaos, suffering and ultimately destruction. They're the natural enemy of good-aligned adventurers. Better yet, they can come back in a new form after being killed. The demon baron the adventurers kill at level 3 can come back to fight them again at level 6 in a new incarnation, or at level 10 in its campaign-ending final form. Demons make great ongoing villains.

DEMONS ARE CONVENIENT

If the adventurers go to where the monsters are, then convenience isn't a problem. A dungeon can be filled with demons just as easily as with orcs, or gelatinous polyhedrons, or murderous gnomish bandits, or zombie griffons. There are monsters out in the wide world. Everyone knows this.

It's when you want the monsters to come to the adventurers that things get tricky. Some monsters need a considerable amount of narrative infrastructure to justify their presence, especially in an urban environment. For example, say you want to run an adventure set in the great city of Axis, where a jealous cousin of the Emperor tries to conquer the Imperial Palace with an army of assassins, only to be thwarted by a plucky band of mismatched adventurers. Your options for that army of assassins are limited. It's unlikely to be an army of orcs—how would orcs get into the city? An army of undead means a lot of scenes of digging around in graveyards or raiding tombs. An army of, say, lizard assassins could be fun, but you still need to work out how to get the lizard men into the city. Half your adventure preparation becomes setting up the logistics of the coup.

However, if it's an army of demons, then all the would-be usurper needs is a demonologist or two and a summoning circle in some basement. You can introduce an army of demons much more easily than an army of orcs or other monsters. You still need to foreshadow the plot—maybe the PCs have to investigate ritual murders, the theft of arcane relics, or a mysterious book stolen from the library at Horizon—but demons bypass lots of pesky questions like "where were all these monsters hiding in the city?"

or "why are we the only ones in position to stop this threat?" If you can't figure out how the bad guys can plausibly accomplish an evil scheme, fill in the gaps with demons.

Demons are the temp agency of evil—whenever you need to add muscle or magic to a sinister plot, call up a demon.

DEMONS ARE EVERYWHERE

Similarly, a Gamemaster can drop in some demons to fight anywhere, in any environment. In the Dragon Empire, you're unlikely to run into an army of orcs when you're down in the Wild Wood, and you probably aren't fighting vampires in the middle of the Kneedeeps. Demons aren't tied to any one region—a hellhole can open anywhere.

Demons are also wonderfully stretchy in terms of power. Most monster concepts have a sweet spot where they 'feel' like the right level. Epic goblins or low-level liches are jarring, but the Abyss spits up level 0 mook demons as well as triple-strength level 15 demon lords.

MAKING DISTINCTIVE DEMONS

Most monsters fit in a particular environment. In a swamp, you're going to fight reptiles, slimes, zombies that try to drown their victims, fog elementals, mushrooms and other icky things. Ice giants or armored dwarves just wouldn't fit. In general, players

are quick to pick up on incongruities. If you add, say, a random gnoll archer to a bunch of human bandits, the players will start speculating about the bandits allying with the gnolls, or assume that gnolls are going to be a big part of the adventure.

But demons fit everywhere. They're like tofu, absorbing flavor from the ingredients around them. If you have a demonologist in a swamp, then she's going to call up mosquito demons and mud demons along with classics like vrocks. You can add a demon to a bunch of bandits just by making one of the bandits a ritual caster.

All that flexibility comes at a cost—it's easy for demons to lose their own schtick and become grab bags of evil powers. Here are some ways to make sure that demons feel like demons, no matter what form they take or where they're encountered.

CHAOTIC AND EVIL

Demons are inherently destructive. They can't help it—they're nothing but entropy and malice and hate. Even when it's not in their ultimate interest to destroy something, they can't resist the urge to smash things and inflict pain. Demons always turn on their summoners; they always turn on each other when there's no-one else to fight, and they always bring ruin to their surroundings.

When describing any area inhabited by demons, emphasize how it's been wrecked and irredeemably tainted. Demons salt the earth by their presence alone. They corrode reality like strong acid.

When describing demonic behavior, emphasize the destructive hatred. Demons are always throwing themselves against the bars of the magical cages; they make time to maim and torture any living things they find, even when that's not the strategically correct option.

MARKS OF THE DEMON

Demons come in a dizzying array of forms, depending on their standing in their native hell-worlds and the substance of their physical shell in the material world. Vulture demons, boar demons, smoke demons, slime demons, fire demons—anything goes. Give these protean horrors some consistency by always having a few demonic 'tells' in your descriptions. For example:

- All demons have glowing red eyes
- Demons stink of sulfur and ash
- Demons cause holy symbols to heat up when nearby
- Fires burn more fiercely and with a weird greenish light in the presence of demons
- Summoned demons always crawl out of tears in reality, and those tears never heal properly.
- When slain, a demon crumples up and collapses in on itself, like a hollow shell getting crushed by external pressure

DEMON'S DICE

All demons (well, other than mooks, and who cares about them) have a chance of having a random demonic ability. You could herald the presence of demons by making a big show of rolling for demonic powers. Don't tell the players what you're rolling—let them work out that "GM cackling and rolling a bunch of d8s in secret behind a screen" equals "we're about to fight a bunch of demons". You could even put aside a few distinctive dice and keep them for demons.

If these ideas appeal to you, you're going to want to see the new list of random demon abilities that appears on page 43.

DEMONIC SPEECH

Demons may vary wildly in their powers and physical appearance, but you could give them a distinctive mode of speech that's consistent across all their many forms. Depending on your tolerance for bad accents and verbal dexterity...

- All demons speak in A HORRIFIC DEEP GUTTERAL GROWLING VOICE
- Order of words the demon scrambles, inherent chaos reflecting in speech distorted. Eyes from your skull remove I; burning of village that is yours then.
- In some tales it's said that demons speak in rhyme, but it hurts my head to do it all the time. Still, a few choice couplets can, experience has shown, distinguish monster from man and set the infernal tone.
- Demons have to blaspheme against the gods. A demon simply cannot say more than a few words without insulting some belief or faith. Cunning demons can try to hide this obligation by picking really obscure religions (Wisdom check to spot that the disguised demon just made a hand gesture that's forbidden by the minor halfling deity Amar the Watcher). Stupid demons, on the other tentacle, are overjoyed by the rise of the Priestess, as now they can insult whole pantheons at once.
- Demons always make reference to their demonic masters in the hells. The infernal hierarchy is in constant flux as one demon lord overthrows another only to be usurped in her turn, but that turbulence makes it even more important for a demon to precisely know its current place in the pack. A demon might introduce itself as *"Zurghal the Despoiler, thirty-fourth demon of the twenty-ninth legion of The Maiden of Scars, who is herself vassal to the Masher of Skulls, second only to Yammoth the Weeping King,"* and be incensed if anyone fails to use its full title.
- Every demon is appointed to destroy a specific place, person or concept. Low-ranking demons might be the bane of a particular apple tree or something extremely obscure (*"I am the cosmic antithesis of the Glitterhaegen Sewer Cleaning Committee"*); more powerful demons have wider portfolios (*"I am the bane of the Elf Queen. I am her destruction, utter and inevitable."*). Demons can destroy other things, but are obsessed with their particular charge.

SYMPATHY FOR THE DIABOLIST; AKA 13 LIES MY DEMON TOLD ME

As tradition—and *13 True Ways*—tell us, devils are the conniving, duplicitous ones who trick us into damning ourselves and demons are the roaring, feral monsters who threaten and bluster.

That's not entirely true. Some demons are quite capable of trickery and honeyed words. The difference is usually that devils can stick to their story, while demons are too chaotic and destructive to maintain a lie for long.

Demons see the world as a prison, and want to break free of it. Here are thirteen ways demons might present that truth speaking directly to followers of specific icons. These stories aren't being told by the icons, they're how a clever demon might address a follower of each of the icons.

A demon might spout one of these tales, then another, or mix and match them, or even grow extra mouths so it can tell many lies at the same time. It'll believe them all, too, while it's telling them. Demons are creatures of the moment, even when that moment is an eternity long and filled with utter hatred for all that exists. Of course you don't necessarily need a story to be true to use its story hooks!

ARCHMAGE

A prison? Yes, and you're in it too. I wish you could remember what it was like before the gods betrayed us and locked us in here. We could do wonders in those days. What you call magic is the smallest trace of that glory, like a brief breath of air that carries the smell of a summer's day into a dark prison cell. When we teach you magic, we teach you to press your face to the bars until you can almost feel the sun on your skin. The gods fear our power, so they keep us all locked up and divided. Clerics and paladins—prison snitches for our jailors.

When we take your soul, think of it as going from one cell block to another. Don't worry—you'll be in our gang. We'll protect you. And we're digging an escape tunnel.

- The Diabolist's cult is rife in Horizon, offering a quicker, easier route to arcane power. One of the wizards of the city hires the adventurers to investigate one of his rivals, who suspects that the rival is consorting with diabolism. The evidence is inconclusive—is someone trying to sow dissent and suspicion in Horizon?
- Agents of the Diabolist storm a fortress dedicated to maintaining the Archmage's wards. Their meddling destabilizes the ward network, making the fortress dangerously unstable. The adventurers must slay the cultists and their demonic guards without causing further damage to the wards. One errant spell could open a new hellhole...

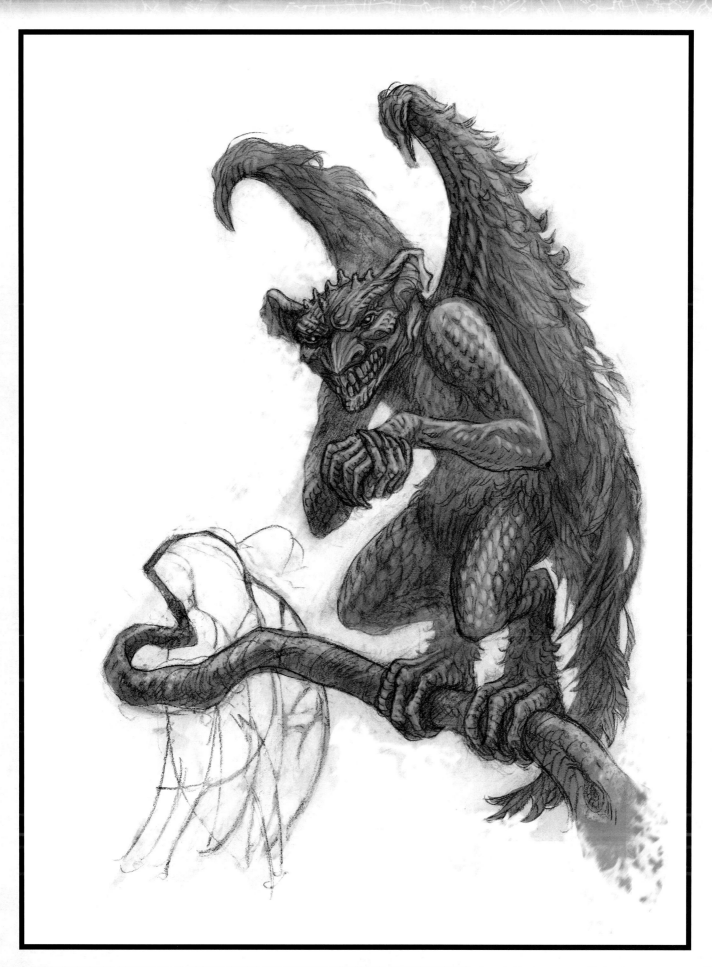

CRUSADER

War is coming. A war with a foe you can't imagine yet, an enemy that is uncreation, unmaking, the antithesis of everything. In that battle, there will only be two sides, for all that is will fight against all that is not (do the math: that means we're outnumbered to the tune of infinity). The world you exist in is not a prison for demons—it's a boot camp. Over all the ages, we've trained you, toughened you, prepared you. It's all right that you hate us and think we're trying to kill you—that's what drill sergeants are for. If you hate my guts, I'm just doing my job right. You'll need that hellfire in your belly when the real enemy arrives.

Deep in your heart, you know this to be true. Every time you fight us, every time you banish us, every hellhole you claim, every swordthrust, what you're really saying is "thank you! Thank you! Thank you! Thank you! Thank you for making me strong! Thank you for making me brave! Thank you for loving me!"

- One of the Crusader's lieutenants comes up with a daring plan. Resurrect a previous Diabolist, causing a civil war in Hell Marsh. An ancient priestess of the Dark Gods has the strength to cast a single *resurrection* spell—all the player characters need to do is bring the old woman into the depths of the Cairnwood and find a suitable tomb to unearth.
- An expedition into the Abyss? Madness—but think of the potential reward. Bring one of the Crusader's iron spikes into the pit and use it to hold back the demons. Sew the wound in the world shut, and the Great Gold Wyrm could return...

DIABOLIST

Imagine the most exquisite puzzle. Imagine a lock as complicated as the world, because it is the world. We're trapped inside it, but you're part of it. If we could get out, we'd... well, there aren't words for what we'd do. We can't open the lock from the inside, and you can't open it from the outside. We can only do it if we work together.

They don't want us to work together. That is why they drove the lesser demons mad, and turned them into monsters—to scare you. That is why they made you think that we are foul and abhorrent and vile—the gods gave you eyes that cannot see our

beauty, and flesh that cannot tolerate our touch. For us to unlock this puzzle and win the prize it holds, you must overcome the weaknesses and fears the gods inflicted on you. You must break through the lies they call sanity and morality and wisdom, lies they sowed so you would not dare reach us.

Reach out. Take my hand. Together, we will break the world.

- The player characters intercept a message from the Diabolist to one of her cultists, warning that a hellhole is about to open near or within a certain town. Do the adventurers bring a warning to the town? Do they report their findings to the Archmage—or the Crusader? Can they stop the hellhole from opening? And perhaps most importantly, did the Diabolist mean for them to intercept the message?

DWARF KING

We call the world a prison we're trying to break out of, but it's more fundamental than that. Mortals create. Demons destroy. These are our essential natures. You mortals are doomed to perish, no matter what you do, so you make things to stave off having to accept the inevitable. You frantically build your little walls against the night, stacking art on babies on nations on money on books on contests, on any legacy that might show you were once, briefly, there. You keep making.

Demons, we're immortal. We can't perish, only change form. We must destroy, as surely as you must create. It's what we are.

So, don't think of what I do as evil. I'm just clearing some space for the next million generations of mortals to build their follies against oblivion.

- The dwarves have lived with the Diabolist on their doorstep for centuries. Hell Marsh is right on the edge of dwarven territory, much closer to Forge than any other city. And if there's one thing dwarves are known for, it's making use of tools. Demons can be just another tool, with the right magic. A clue, perhaps, to the origins of derro?
- A secret dwarf smelting technique requires flames that burn hotter than any fuel can muster. In Ages past, the dwarves captured dragons, but now a heretical cabal of smiths plot to use hellfire as a power source. Could an alliance between the Diabolist and Dwarf King provide enough magical weapons to break the Orc Lord's armies?

ELF QUEEN

As above, so below. You have lived long enough to see these patterns repeat. You've seen a thousand thousand sunrises, and know that dusk will come again. You've seen winter yield to spring and back again as the years wheel by. You know there will be ages after ages, history repeating itself in new forms.

The three shards of elf-kind—dark, wood and high—unite in the Elf Queen. So too, then, there are three shards of being. There are creatures of the underworld, which you call demons. Creatures of the middle world, such as yourselves. And creatures of the overworld, all united in a divinity you cannot perceive because you are part of it. You are like the wood elves, flighty and merry. We demons are like the dark elves—we do things that seem unwholesome and terrible, but they are necessary, and we are commanded to do them by the All-Queen.

We are your cousins. Together, we both serve the true Queen.

- *The dark elves have their own schools of demonology. They cultivate trees of woe, which draw up demonic spirits through their roots. These demons manifest as faces on the tree-trunks, and slowly, slowly they grow bodies of thorn and insects and leaf-mold for themselves. These demons may take many years to grow, but they are more loyal and easier to control. What happens when the High Druid learns of this magical perversion of her trees?*

- *The Diabolist and the Elf Queen have much in common. Both are aloof and mysterious, both virtually immortal. Both wield arcane power that rivals that of the Archmage. Both have a dark side they must control—the Queen has her drow, the Diabolist her demons. Could the Diabolist emulate the Queen by summoning creatures of the overworld, becoming the Thaumaturgist and balancing light and darkness?*

EMPEROR

Order! Law! Control! Yes, that's all very good, very impressive indeed. Enforce that iron will of yours on an Empire of warring factions. Keep the peace through diplomacy and honorable deeds—backed up by those legions of fiery dragons, of course.

The thing is—and forgive me for pointing this out—your "law" and "justice" stem from the sword, don't they? The sword and the dragon's breath? The Emperor is the emperor because one of his ancestors cast down the Wizard King. The whole Imperial dynasty's founded on might making right. Nothing wrong with that at all—I'm a demon, I'm all about equating power with truth and rightness. I just object to cloaking the self-evident truth that the Emperor's rule is founded on the power to do brutal slaughter in words like "justice" and "law".

Not that there's much justice in the Empire, these days. You know that the Emperor's weak, don't you? His advisers and viziers are running the show for their own ends. The Archmage is running wild down in Horizon, doing all sorts of terrible experiments against the natural order, while over in the Wild Wood they're oppressing the peaceful followers of the High Druid. Not much justice there? And honor? Haven't you noticed there's a BLUE DRAGON of all things running one of the seven cities? How much of a bribe do you think she paid?

Now, you seem like a good adventurer. You must be—you're off risking your life to fight demons. But, friend, the truth is that you're defending a rotten dynasty. The Emperor's as bad as the Wizard King ever was, he's just better at hiding it. What we need is another hero to step up and fight for truth and justice and freedom. A real hero, a legendary champion who'll cast down the false Emperor and drive out corruption and evil. Someone with the courage and conviction to break the world and remake it again. Make it better this time.

What's that you say? You're a heroic adventurer? Well, you'll need an army—and I happen to have a lot of friends with very, very big teeth.

- *The Crusader is—in theory—a sworn servant of the Emperor, and the Crusader knows secret ways to control demons. Could demons be used to augment the Empire's forces as they battle the Orc Lord and the undead?*

- *The city of Axis has been destroyed and rebuilt several times. The first city, for example, was razed by giants. Another incarnation of the city was destroyed by a volcanic eruption—although the Oracle of that Age suggested it was a divine punishment for demon-worship. In past Ages, demons were everywhere in the Empire, summoned by ambitious wizards and used for all manner of sinister purposes. Now, archaeologists and treasure hunters have begun to excavate the ruins of that demonic city. What will they find in the grave of Emperors?*

GREAT GOLD WYRM

A paladin of the Golden Order? Truly? My word... can I just say, before we battle, what a tremendous honor is it to meet you? Really, we're all very impressed Down There with you paladins. I mean, we have it easy. Destruction and ravening and burning things down, that comes naturally. Us demons, we're just playing to our base instincts. We don't need discipline or self-denial or courage or anything—we just do what we feel like. We just have fun.

But you! A whole lifetime of self-sacrifice and iron discipline! Keeping yourself pure and noble and true to those holy teachings all the time! And it's not like the pay's any good. I mean, people may respect paladins, but they don't like them, for the most part. You scare them. You show them how far they are from goodness, how much they'd have to give up to be holy like you. You make people uncomfortable.

I honestly don't know how you keep going. It must be so very hard, especially as you're not getting anywhere. Thwart one demonic invasion, and there'll be another one next week. You give up your whole life just to keep the status quo, and no-one's even going to remember your sacrifice in a few years. I mean, what's your end-game? What's your victory condition? "Everyone comes together in joy and peace and evil is gone forever?"

Tell me, how likely is that? Who do you think is closer to winning the war, your side or mine?

The Great Gold Wyrm knew. He knew he was losing. Oh yes, he lied to you. "I'm just going to block this hellhole with my body, that'll work." Nonsense. He gave up. Committed suicide. Took the easy way out. All those dreams and portents, they're just echoes. Whispers from a guilty ghost who wanted to stop struggling, but didn't want to be held responsible for his side's ultimate defeat.

He's gone, but you're still here. Still fighting the good fight. Still tilting at those windmills. As I said, everyone Down Below admires you. We wouldn't have the courage to do what you do.

Of course, we don't need to. We're the easy side. And we only need to win once to break free.

- A demon approaches a player character of the Golden Order, and claims that the influence of the Wyrm has convinced it to atone for its demonic ways. Can the player character be a moral guardian for the demon—or is this a trick?

- Ages ago, the Diabolist worked perhaps the greatest and most terrible act of demon summoning in history. She opened the Abyss, and would have destroyed the world if it were not for the Great Gold Wyrm's sacrifice. Only two beings know how she did—the Diabolist herself, and the Great Gold Wyrm, who saw her ritual as she completed it. That knowledge may still be locked in the rotting brain of the icon's corpse. Anyone feel like a combined necromantic ritual/drilling expedition/dungeon crawl into the Abyss?

High Druid

It's easy to get caught in the cycles. Summer follows spring, autumn follows summer, then winter and back again. Sun rises, sun sets. Planting and harvest, life and death and rebirth. You can get lulled to sleep by the endless repetition of the natural world. Hypnotized, even.

The High Druid says demons are unnatural, that we're not a part of the world. The truth is that it's the world that's unnatural. When you feel truly alive—when you're sitting on a hillside, watching the same dumb sheep getting fat for the thousandth time, or when you're standing on a mountaintop with a storm raging around you, the wind and rain lashing your face, the thunder echoing in your blood? Nature at its purest is about change, adaptation, destruction and creation in wild new forms, not the prison routine of the "natural" cycles.

Who said autumn has to follow summer? Why can't it be spring a hundred times in a row until you finally find the right one?

The cycle's a lie. The High Druid's a liar. Break it. Break her.

- In past Ages, before the rise of the Crusader, it was the High Druid who vied with the Diabolist. Nature is an expression of the physical world, the world that the demons seek to destroy. There are trees growing in the deep wood that are living wards, their root systems intertwining across hundreds of miles to bind reality together. The Wizard King's wards were made in arcane imitation of these living wards. If the current High Druid were able to recreate these trees and sow them across the world, she could end the threat from the demons.

- The Middle Sea is home to many demons, who were caught in the spell that tamed the ocean. These demons are now trapped on little islands scattered across the waters. If the High Druid succeeds in her aim of freeing the sea called Stormmaker, those demons will also be freed—unless, say, a band of heroic demon slayers set sail to cleanse the ocean first.

Lich King

We were enemies once. In Ages past, long ago, the Wizard King brought order out of chaos and drove the demons back screaming beyond the walls of the world. You think the Archmage's wards are powerful? You should have seen the wards back then! (I couldn't—I'm a demon, and my eyes would have melted if I'd dared peak at the Wizard King's works).

Things have changed since then. Now, the Wizard King is the Lich King, the king of the dead. And the dead are great! Super-great! No-one's as loyal as a zombie, that's what I always say. The Necropolis is the best-run city in the Empire—no crime, no unhappiness, no sickness, no injustice. The problem is all the living people, right? Demons and undead, we can both take the long view, and from that perspective, you can see the truth—mortals are horrible. They're self-deluding, violent, nasty little things without any real sense of higher purpose. It'd be much better for the Empire if everyone in it was undead and ruled by the Lich King.

Us demons, we're on-board with that plan. Kill 'em all and let the Lich King sort it out. Once the Lich King's back in his rightful place in charge of the Empire, you can rebuild those wards and lock us demons out again, so it's win/win for the dead. We just want to have some fun slaughtering people for a good cause, just like adventurers.

So let us in. Let the armies of Hell march under the banner of the true Emperor for once.

- Those previous Diabolists in their tombs in the Cairnwood? Ever hear of better candidates for retroactive lichdom?

Orc Lord

There's demon blood in the Orc Lord. That's how the elves made him, of course. They wove mortal and demon essence together and birthed the first orc. The Orc Lord is an honorary prince of hell, our most beloved half-mortal Cousin, of equal rank with the Diabolist in the lowerarchy. That's why demons are so willing to fight for the Orc Lord, or to be summoned by his shamans and war-wizards. We're family.

Now, the same spells that made the Orc Lord bind him and imprison him. The elves were tricksy and clever—they put geases into those spells, making it physically impossible for the Orc Lord to know his own true nature. He can't accept the truth that he's a demon lord bound in mortal form. He can't break free of the prison of his own flesh.

You've got to bust him out. If you free the Orc Lord, he'll have the strength he needs to conquer the Empire. An unbound Orc Lord would be unstoppable and invincible, but he'll never know his own power unless you break the ancient shackles the elves put on him.

- The Orc Lord and the Diabolist must come to an arrangement, or come to blows. His armies march relentlessly south, and Hellmarsh is on his left flank as he advances. The Diabolist, as always, plays both sides, inviting both the Empire and the Orcs to send diplomats to her court. Who offers her more?
- If orcs are demons, and the presence of orcs creates half-orcs, then does the presence of demons create half-demons? Or does this magical effect require experimentation to unlock its potential?

Priestess

Just so we're absolutely clear—over there we've got the Crusader. The Fist of the Dark Gods. The greatest fighter and general in this Age of the world, with the possible exception of the Orc Lord. And he's sworn to destroy us demons. More than that, he's worked out a way to cap our hellholes with his fortresses and add our power to his. Every time he defeats the forces of Hell, he gets stronger, and so do his Dark Gods.

And over here, we've got the Priestess, who's terribly nice. She has a very pretty cathedral, and a very pretty smile, and she makes you feel all fuzzy and warm.

Tell me, friend, what is she going to do when the Crusader conquers the last hellhole and turns his gaze towards Santa Cora? What happens when an uncountable legion of battle-hardened bastard cut-throats, enslaved demons, mutant horrors and cultists of the Dark Gods march on the Cathedral? What's the Priestess's response going to be, a group prayer session? Even if the Light is the equal of the Dark, the Crusader's ability to seize control of demons tips the balance towards the bad guys. It's not going to be the Priestess and the Gods of Light versus the Crusader and the Dark Gods, it's going to be the Priestess and her gods against the Crusader, his gods, and all the demons he's enslaved.

You could help. You could save the Priestess, maybe even save the world. All you need to do is work out how to break the Crusader's binding spells...

- Demons see the world as an ever-changing, infinitely complex and incredibly resilient prison, a giant shell of imperishable crystal, a lock without a key. Does that sound like the Cathedral to anyone else? Is the Priestess building a demon trap? Or is she trying to contain the power of all the Light?

Prince of Shadows

You think it's a coincidence that your Prince's stronghold is in Shadowport, just down the river from the Hellmarsh? Do you think it's vanity that made the Prince hide his true name under a showy title? Did you assume that the Prince wants only mundane anarchy, that he defies only the laws of the Empire and its cities and magistrates?

No, the Prince is one of us. There's a demon under that hood, and he breaks not only the laws of the Empire, but the laws of reality and sanity too. Do you envy his mad cavalcade of indulgence and trickery as he roams the world? You can have that too, if you let us help you?

And as for his true mission—thieves are very good at picking locks and breaking out of prisons. Everything the Prince of Shadows does brings us one step closer to escaping the jail of the world. He's our man on the inside of reality, our second-world burglar.

- The Prince's alliance with the Diabolist benefits both of them, but neither trusts the other. He gets magical support and demonic muscle when he needs it; she gets access to a network of spies and couriers, allowing her to maintain contact with all her cultists and agents across the world. If the Diabolist were to open a hellhole in Shadowport, she'd have a metaphorical knife at the Prince's throat. All it needs is sufficient bloodshed. . . .
- A demon named Bloodflood escaped the Diabolist's control and fled down the coast to Shadowport. Now, he's one of the most feared pirates on the Midland Sea. There's a reward for slaying Bloodflood, but how much more treasure could you obtain if you bound Bloodflood and forced him to reveal where he's buried all his loot?

The Three

Hey, you with the Blue? You got suckered. You're trapped the same way we are. Demons are locked inside reality, and you're locked inside the Empire. You might think you've got the upper hand, but the truth is you're caught just like we are. The oaths and geases will bind the Blue tighter and tighter until she's the Emperor's lap-dragon. The only thing to do is break free. You've got all that sorcerous power and magic might—maybe whip up a chain-breaking spell of escape. Let us help you!

Hey, you with the Black? You live in a swamp and do forbidden, unholy things—us too! We can help one another. Swim on over to Hellmarsh sometime, and let's make some evil schemes to overthrow the Empire.

Hey, you with the Red? You like fire? We like fire, too, a whole lot.

Let's burn.

- The Blue is one of the most accomplished demonologists in the Empire, although her expertise is second to the Diabolist herself. If the Diabolist agrees to set up a school of demonology in Drakkenhall, it would set the city on a path to becoming a dark mirror of Horizon, a second city of wonders on the far side of the Midland Sea. What can the Blue offer the Diabolist as a token of friendship?

THE ECOLOGY OF THE HELLHOLE

Here's the ecology of hellhole, from first eruption to final threat. As you'll see in the next chapter, there are many possible exceptions to this general story!

BEGINNINGS

Here's how you make a hellhole.

First, you find a place where reality's already weak. Some such places occur naturally. There are cosmic fissures, elemental junctures, soft places, magical borderlands. Other places are inflicted like wounds. A magical catastrophe, a mass slaughter or the worm-trail of a living dungeon could all weaken reality enough for the purposes of a hellhole.

Second, you need to conduct an arcane ritual. A very big arcane ritual, involving lots of sacrifices and magical power. It's the same sort of spell you use to summon a demon, but instead of calling up a named demon, you're opening the way for all of them. Alternatively, if there's enough magical energy sloshing around nearby, it may pool in the weak spot in reality and erode the fabric of existence until it frays through into a hellhole. (Maybe that's where most of the Hellmarsh hellholes come from—backwash from the Diabolist's experiments).

Three, stand well back, because if your ritual works, you don't want to be standing there when the hellhole opens.

At the dead center of every hellhole (well . . . . *most* hellholes) is a gate to the hells or to the Abyss. There aren't any binding circles or containment pentagrams around that gate, so the chaotic energies of the demon realm leech through into our reality, warping space and time. As long as that gate stays open, the hellhole exists in all its impossibility; the bigger the gate grows, the bigger the hellhole.

'Bigger' is relative, by the way. Hellholes mangle space like demons mangle the flesh of the innocents, stretching it and piercing it and tying it knots and and eating it and bleeding it. A hellhole might be only a mile or two across, but contain whole continents of carnage. They do the same to time—a minute in a hellhole might be a minute on the outside, or a second, or a day, or ten thousand years. (The bigger the distortion, the more unstable the hellhole, so it's rare to get really egregious insults to space and time.)

THE FIRST HOURS

Demons crawl out of the gate as soon as it's opened. Small demons wriggle through the instant the gate is opened. For a small demon, a dretch or imp or some other hellscum, getting through a hellhole is a once-in-eternity triumph, as they can establish themselves on the far side of the gate before the bigger, nastier demons come through.

Demons don't have a fixed shape. A nalfeshnee doesn't 'really' look like a hairy winged boar; a vrock isn't actually a vulture-monster. Those are shapes imposed on them by the spells used to summon them, or by the rules of reality. Hellholes obey different rules, so demons may have other forms there. A dretch looks like a cringing blob of slime when summoned into existence in the outside world, but when it comes through a newly opened hellhole, it can take on a new and more powerful shape borrowed from its surroundings. Open a hellhole in a forest, and you'll get demons stealing the shapes of trees and nettles and wolves and bunnies. Open one in a court, and you'll get demon lawyers wearing wigs and masked demon executioners with head-chopping axes. Demons treat the world like a two-year old treats a dress-up box full of explosives.

Anyone in the hellhole in this initial phase is in trouble. When demons come through the gate, they gain physical form, including physical stomachs and the hunger to fill them. If you're not eaten, it's probably because you were standing in the wrong place and got fused with a demon as it clawed its way into the material realm.

STABILIZATION

After that initial mad rush, the hellhole and its denizens come to some sort of equilibrium. The gate stops growing once it reaches its fullest sustainable size. The demons fight amongst themselves until the strongest one comes out on top, becoming the ruler of the hellhole. The laws of physics and magic in this pocket dimension settle down, becoming at least vaguely predictable.

This is the time when the hellhole is most vulnerable. If you're a heroic adventurer, now's the time to plunge into the pit and fight your way to the exposed and unprotected gate at the heart of the hellhole. Close that gate, and the hellhole collapses. If you're an evil demonologist (perhaps the same one who opened the hellhole), then you can tap that unprotected gate and turn it into a wellspring of magical power.

FORTIFICATION

Demons don't agree on much. They argue about the optimal number of limbs, they disagree on how to cook halflings, they dicker on the value of souls, and they murder each other over the most inane or trifling insults. They do, however, agree that hellholes should be defended. As soon as they can, they build defenses and traps to protect their new outpost in the mortal world. Sometimes, the biggest demon becomes king of the hellhole and builds (carves/conjures/secretes/grows/turns into) a fortress on top of the gate to protect it. More frequently, the demons form gangs or factions and war over control of the gate.

RAIDING

Now that the demons have a secure foothold in the mortal world, their instinctive, unquenchable hatred of existence drives them to hurt everything around them. Hosts of demons swarm out of the hole to lay waste to the lands around; vile pestilences and chaotic storms of magic boil out of the hole to bring ruin and suffering. Fortunately for the rest of existence, demons cannot survive for long outside the hellhole's magical zone of chaos. If they go too far, the pressure of stable reality crushes them into non-existence or forces them to retreat. Demons make terrible and noisy neighbors, but it's possible to live close to a hellhole in relative safety (until a breed of tougher or faster demon shows up, a type that can make it from the hellhole's edge to your front door before it has to retreat).

It's much easier to cede the few miles of territory around a hellhole to the demons and let it go to waste rather than mount a siege of a fortified hellhole. The various long-lasting hellholes scattered around the eastern and southern regions of the Dragon Empire are all far enough away from anywhere important that the official Imperial policy is to leave them alone, to cordon them off and contain them instead of attacking them (a policy the Crusader, obviously, ignores).

Contraction

The Archmage protects the Empire with a network of magical protective wards, and one of the chief purposes of these wards is to stop hellholes expanding. These wards reinforce the natural pressure of reality, keeping the demons penned up inside their self-made prisons. Over centuries, if the wards are maintained and kept fully charged, they can even squeeze the hellhole gates shut, destroying the hellholes completely. Without these wards, the Archmage claims that the hellholes would continue to widen and widen, until all the world falls into hell.

While the Archmage's wards are an astounding boon for the Empire, they are immensely costly and increasingly hard to defend. Some even suspect that the Archmage is wrong—there are places outside the Empire that are not under the aegis of his wards, and those lands have not (as far as anyone knows) fallen under the control of demons. This suggests that the wounds in reality heal naturally, and that a hellhole will close of its own accord after a few centuries instead of growing until it consumes the world.

A few heretical theorists from Horizon even argue that the wards are ultimately making matters worse; they argue that all the 'closed' hellholes will pop open in unison if those wards ever fail, and that the Empire would be better served tolerating a few more hellholes instead of building up a lake of woe behind a magical dam.

It should be noted that the Hell Marsh of the Diabolist is *outside* the currently active wards. The Hell Marsh region is technically part of the Empire, but has been left to fall into anarchy and ruin for a good long while, perhaps even Ages. The hellholes there grow unchecked—so time may tell which theory is correct.

Demon Stats

This section opens with a second look at random demon abilities and ends with monster stats for the demons introduced by the demonologist's summoning spells.

Random Demon Abilities

RH speaking . . . . As the designer of the original Random Demon Abilities table, I'm fond of the idea but not the execution. The problem with the earlier table (as found on page 209 of the *13th Age* core rulebook) is that several of the abilities it generates are either not relevant to most fights or not particularly fun. Use that previous list whenever you feel like it, or try this new version if you're comfortable with demon abilities that may have more of an impact.

Random determination: If you want to keep things random, roll a d10 for each non-mook normal-sized demon. If you roll less than or equal to its level, the demon has a random ability, roll a d6 or d8 on the table below. Large or huge (or double-strength and triple-strength) demons automatically have one random ability.

No overload: Alternatively, if a battle is full of demons, choose one or two demons you care about most to get a random (or not) special ability. You know how involved you want battles to be, so choose the number of extra abilities you'll deal with instead of letting the dice decide.

New Random Demon Abilities (d6 or d8)

1: *Deathwish*—The demon takes a −2 penalty to all defenses and gains a +3 attack bonus.

2: *Entropic warp*—When an enemy deals miss damage to the demon, that enemy also takes half that amount of damage.

3: *Bad ending*—While staggered, the demon gains a +2 bonus with its attacks.

4: *Big hate*—Each battle, the demon gains a +4 attack bonus until the end of the battle against the first enemy that hits it with an attack.

5: *Loophole*—When the demon starts its turn with 10 hit points or fewer, it can teleport out of the battle as a move action. If it does it will return to face the PCs *soon*. Add the full-strength demon to an upcoming battle as a nasty complication to an upcoming battle, having it teleport in during the first or second round of combat. (Champion tier: 25 hp or fewer; epic tier: 50 hp or fewer).

6: *Teleport 1d3 times each battle*—As a move action, the demon can teleport anywhere it can see nearby.

7: *Demonic speed*—The demon can take an extra action each turn while the escalation die is 4+.

8: *Theft of fate*—At the start of each round, the demon rolls a hard save. If the save succeeds, it steals the escalation die that round, adding the escalation die to its own attacks but preventing the PCs from adding the die to their attacks.

New Demons

The hellhole write-ups in chapter 3 also contain many new demon stat blocks, but most of the demons in chapter 3 are creatures of specific situations and hellhole terrain. The demons below are somewhat more generic creatures who have proven susceptible to demonologists' summoning spells.

SIX HELLHOLES

SIX HELLHOLES

This chapter provides playable or inspiring details details on specific hellholes that don't always match the approach taken by our notes on generic hellholes. Here's what hellholes are: chaotic. Here's what they're not: predictable.

We'll talk about each hellhole's denizens, its weird environmental conditions, its dangers, its opportunities and give some reasons beyond suicidal madness for a band of adventurers to enter such a place. What we won't talk about is a hellhole's exact location or complete history (or if we do, nothing we say should be taken as immutable). Mix and match these hellholes as thoroughly as you wish. Be both chaotic and unpredictable to your players—keep them guessing.

The six hellholes detailed below show the full range of demonic threats, from woodland nuisance to cosmic threat.

Page 46: **Ratwood** (levels 1-2). A small but growing leftover of a hellhole that was believed to have been destroyed . . .

Page 49: **High Heath of Unending Woe** (levels 2-3). A nasty place to get stuck. Getting out will take time and many encounters, most of which are written up as playable scenes and battles.

Page 61: **Claw Peak** (levels 3-4). A strange hellhole with somewhat divided denizens and an uneasy leader. Battles are discussed rather than statted-out, there's room for several different approaches to this problem area.

Page 64: **Floating Market** (Any levels): This isn't a hellhole you're meant to enter and fight. Yes, there is a hellhole here, but it's hidden well, and the town built around the hellhole is a place where humans and demons mingle in ways that would be unthinkable anywhere else.

Page 70: **Red Crag Castle** (levels 5-6): Sometimes demons are their own worst enemies. The demon factions struggling for control of a castle they've turned into a hellhole aren't likely to cooperate effectively, so the PCs may be able to face-down overwhelming odds, or at least accomplish a mission or two and get out alive.

Page 79: **Hellgout** (levels 8-10): Epic tier! The Abyss erupts into the overworld. The center cannot hold.

THE RATWOOD

Location: Anywhere in the Empire
Level Range: 1-2 (Adventurer-tier)

Old men in the village tell stories passed down from their grandmothers about how the Ratwood was once the Wood of Hungry Thorns, a terrible hellhole ruled by a demon king. Long long ago (in the days of the Wizard King, they say, but every story of long ago starts that way, and it's likely this tale dates to the 12th Age and not the 1st), heroes came up from Axis and braved the perils of the Hungry Thorns, and slew the demon king, and drove the demons back to hell. And yea, then they went to the village tavern, and spent hard-won demons' gold on a round of beers for the whole village and there was much rejoicing—so ever since, it's tradition that wandering adventurers who visit the village buy a round of drinks for the old men who tell this story. Mine's a dwarven ale, thanks very much.

What the story doesn't mention and the villagers don't know is that the job was left half-done. The hellhole was imperfectly sealed, leaving a small crack no bigger than a hairsbreadth.

But even the width of a single hair is enough for some demons. Hell is seeping back into the world. Only the weakest demons can fit through the crack, so they've made bodies for themselves from the vermin of the woods, from rats and beetles and crows, from leaf mould and nettles and thorn bushes.

So far, the demons haven't accomplished much. They can ruin harvests, spread disease, terrify the occasional passer-by, and lure a lost child or two into the woods. What they need is a spellcaster—a sorcerer or a wizard or a demonologist who can widen the crack and reopen the hellhole . . . .

HOOKS

- The demons of the Ratwood send a crow messenger to the fortress of the Diabolist, offering to serve her for a hundred years if she sends them a sorcerer to open the hellhole. The Crusader's spies discover this plot, and send the adventurers to intercept the Diabolist's agent on the road.
- Some other business brings the adventurers to the village. Seeing an opportunity, the demons kidnap a child from the village and send the adventurers a message—open the dormant hellhole or the child dies.
- The unquiet ghost of one of the previous adventurers appears to a player character in a dream, and confesses that they left the job half-done. Guilt gnawed at her soul all her life, and followed her into death. She cannot rest until the hellhole is fully sealed.

PERILS

- **Wicked Thorns:** Cruel thorns that cut and stab when you try to pass through. +10 vs AC; take 2d10 damage, or take 2d4 and get so stuck that the rest of the party has to spend up to an hour cutting you free.
- **Fouled Supplies:** Malicious demon rats sneak into your backpack to eat, defile and leave insulting critiques of your rations. Make a Constitution skill check (DC20) to avoid the pangs of hunger costing you a recovery.
- **Marsh Gas:** Wisps, then clouds of glowing gas seep up from the ground, making the whole forest seem dreamlike and eerie (and foul-smelling). Make a Wisdom check (DC20) to avoid getting lost and separated from the rest of the party.

DENIZENS

Demon rats are everywhere in the Ratwood—underfoot in the underbrush, dropping from branches overhead to gnaw on an unguarded eyeball, creeping into your bedroll at night to slit your throat. Ratwood terrors are rarer, found only in the deepest and darkest dells of the forest. And there's only one Thorn King, a demon that's possessed a great hawthorn tree that's grown over the mostly-sealed central gate.

RANDOM RATWOOD DEMON ABILITIES (D4)

As usual, mooks generally don't have a random demon ability, though you could make an exception. If you want the dice to decide, normal sized demons have a random demon ability if you roll equal or less than their level on a d10. Large demons like the Thorn King most always have a random demon ability.

1: *Camouflage*—the demon starts the encounter invisible
2: *Barkskin*—the demon gains Resist Damage 16+
3: *Terrain Stunt*—the demon can perform a terrain stunt once per battle, as per the ranger talent (*13th Age*, p. 120)
4: *Turn to Rats*—when first staggered, the demon falls apart into a swarm of 1d4+1 demon rats. When all the rats are slain, it reappears immediately.

DEMON RAT

Take a rat. Pull it inside out. Give it strange paws like furry human hands, and a face full of demon malice. Repeat five hundred times and swarm.

0th level mook [DEMON]
Initiative: +4

Gnaw +5 vs. AC—3 damage

R: Tiny shortbow +4 vs. AC—3 damage

Scuttle and hide: Attacks against demon rats suffer a −2 attack penalty if the attacker is not engaged with the rat mob.

AC	16	
PD	14	**HP 5 (mook)**
MD	10	

Mook: Kill one demon rat mook for every 5 damage you deal to the mob.

RATWOOD TERROR

There's nothing there, just a darkness under the ivy-laden trees. Just a miasma in the air. Just an overwhelming sense of terror. This place is not for you.

3rd level spoiler [DEMON]
Initiative: +6

Claws +8 vs. AC—10 damage
  Special: This attack can only target a foe taking ongoing psychic damage from *terror of the grove.*

C: Terror of the grove +8 vs MD (all nearby enemies)—5 psychic damage, plus 5 ongoing psychic damage (save ends)
  Special: This attack cannot target foes already taking psychic damage.

Shade of the grove: The Ratwood terror is ghostly (*resist damage 16+*) and invisible (50% miss chance) to all foes except those who took psychic damage from it since their last turn. (In other words, foes who have been hit by terror of the grove since their last turn can see and attack the terror normally, but others cannot!)

Nastier Specials
Fear: Enemies that have 15 hp or fewer engaged with the Ratwood terror suffer from fear (−4 attack penalty and lose the escalation die).

AC	17	
PD	13	**HP 38**
MD	16	

Thorn King

Half-demon, half-tree, all nasty.

Large 3rd level wrecker [DEMON]
Initiative: +6

Swiping branches +8 vs. AC (2 attacks)—9 damage
Natural 16+: The target is afflicted by *crown of thorns* (normal save ends, 11+)

R: Hail of thorns +8 vs PD (1d4+1 nearby or far away enemies)—4d6 damage

Crown of thorns: A character afflicted by a *crown of thorns* takes damage whenever he or she attacks the thorn king. The damage starts at 10 and increases by 5 for every subsequent attack (15 for the second attack, 20 for the third and so forth).

Immobile: The Thorn King cannot move.

Nastier Specials

Burning tree: When the Thorn King becomes staggered for the first time, it catches fire. Add +1d6 fire damage to his *swiping branches*, and the king may now make a number of *swiping branches* attacks equal to the escalation die (minimum 2 attacks). He also takes 2d6 fire damage each round until destroyed.

AC	20	
PD	16	**HP 100**
MD	15	

HIGH HEATH OF UNENDING WOE

Location: Anywhere in the Empire
Level Range: 2-3

The high heath is a region of moorland that extends from wherever you to put in your campaign all the way to another location in your campaign. The heath makes for poor farmland, despite the efforts of previous Archmages (titanic fallen stones, the remnants of ancient elemental workings, dot the barren landscape). A road crosses the moor between those two previously-mentioned locations, wending past the low hills and rocky outcrops that rise from the heather. Other than a few sheep and goats, there are few signs of life on the high heath, although there are stories of bandits and worse things—giants, wyverns and manticores are most commonly mentioned in tales by the fire. These tales say talk of how brave heros slew the monsters, or canny travelers escaped them, or fools fell prey to them.

The stories also warn of the hellhole called Unending Woe, but on this topic the stories are vague. There is a place on the high heath that looks like all the rest, another landscape of low brown bushes and stony hills, but if you set foot there, you shall never return.

The high heath hellhole is an insult to cartographers. All hellholes play games with distance, but Unending Woe does so to an absurd degree. Once a traveler passes the invisible edge of the hellhole, the lands stretch around them almost infinity, and they are doomed to wander for days, weeks, or even longer. If they try to retrace their steps, they find themselves walking endlessly without any forward progress. Trying to leave the hellhole by walking out is like Zeno's Paradox—a traveler can go infinitely close to the edge without ever reaching it.

The only way out is through the middle. Those trapped in the hellhole eventually turn inwards, marching towards the center. By the time they reach the inner region of the hellhole, where the barren heath gives way to more traditional lakes-of-sulfur and forbidding-spiky-fortresses, most trapped victims give themselves willingly to the demons, having been driven mad by their endless wanderings.

The Empire, of course, is aware of the danger posed by Unending Woe. There have been numerous attempts to mark the boundaries of the hellhole, but those boundaries flow like invisible poison. One day, that hill is safe; next day, if you set foot on that hill, you might as well be on the moon. A platoon of Imperial Legion engineers sent to place marker stones lost half its number by mischance when the boundary advanced suddenly. The doomed soldiers were still visible to their comrades, standing only a few feet away, but a virtually infinite gulf separated them. Those on the inside could have marched for years and come no closer to escaping; those on the outside could have taken a few steps forward to reach their friends, but then they would have been caught too.

The Archmage has promised to develop a reliable divination spell that can precise mark the boundaries of Unending Woe, but his to-do list is long.

HOOKS

- The Archmage believes he's developed a magical gemstone that, when looked through, reveals the boundaries of Unending Woe. He sent the gemstone with a courier to the Imperial Legion fort closest to the hole. Unfortunately, the courier was ambushed by bandits, and they've fled up onto the heath. Find them before they accidentally cross into the hellhole.
- A shepherd returns to the nearest town with an astounding tale. While hunting for a lost lamb, she found a narrow defile that runs deep into the hellhole, but isn't affected by the hellhole's warping of distance. Better yet, she's sure that she saw a wyvern's cave at the end of the defile. Maybe it's stuffed with treasure. She'll show the adventurers where it is in exchange for a share of the booty.
- In accordance with her oath to the Emperor, the Blue sent a detachment of monstrous troops from Drakkenhall to fight on the frontier against the orcs. However, her troops vanished on the road while crossing the high heath. Did they blunder into the hellhole? Were they ambushed by enemies of the Three who want to stop the Blue from gaining more influence in the Empire? Is this part of some stratagem to smuggle monsters into the Empire along the Emperor's own roads? It's up to the adventurers to find out what became of the Blue Legion.

PERILS

Unending Woe is one big peril. Once you cross the hellhole's boundary, you can't walk back out as the distance stretches like rubber. *Teleporting* might work, or it might smear you across the landscape. It's almost impossible to tell where the edge of the hellhole starts; careful examination of the movements of birds and insects or exceptionally keen magical divinations might give it away (DC30 either way).

The only reliable way to escape the hellhole is to go to the center and find a way out through there.

HUNGER & THIRST

13th Age doesn't normally bother with tracking rations, waterskins, shelter and other supplies. It's assumed that the player characters are hardened travelers who know how to take care of themselves in the wild. The high heath, though, is notoriously barren and exposed, and the adventurers may be trapped here for a long time. If the adventurers wander for a long period, have the character with the best wilderness-survival type background make a skill check (initially DC15, rising by +5 for each check.) two or three times during their wanderings. If that adventurer fails the check, everyone loses a recovery. Those without a recovery to spend pay the usual consequences (*13th Age* core rulebook, page 169).

SINKHOLES

These open unexpectedly beneath adventurers. Single target, +15 vs. PD, 3d6 damage if you fall in.

LIGHTNING STORMS

These crash unexpectedly on top of adventurers. Multiple targets, +15 vs. PD, 1d12 damage if you're sent flying by winds, deafened by thunder, or menaced by lightning.

RANDOM DEMON ABILITIES OF UNENDING WOE (D4)

Feel free to use either the original random demon ability table or the new table on page 43, or use this table for a touch of the Heath's woe.

1: *Cold Wind*—The demon starts the combat insubstantial, as a shadow on the wind. In this form, it moves at double speed and has Resist weapons 18+. The demon materializes for the rest of the battle when it attacks or when the escalation die reaches 2.

2: *Malice*—If the demon crits, it also reduces the target's number of remaining recoveries by 1.

3: *Aura of Despair*—Characters with a number of remaining recoveries equal to or less than the demon's level feel despair when engaged with the demon. Despairing characters suffer a −4 penalty to attacks against the demon and don't get to use the escalation die.

4: *Teleport* 1d3 times per battle

OLD HILL GIANTS

They've been expecting the adventurers.

The heath is a sacred ground for the hill giants—old hill giants, too old to defend their caves, get driven into this empty land to die. There are long mounds everywhere where giants of old sank into the soil. The Old Hill Giants are frail and half-blind, but the hellhole lends them a little demonic strength so that it can claim their souls when they perish.

As 4th level monsters go they're weak. That's appropriate for a minor combat the PCs may not even get full credit for and as a sign of how bad things can get here in the heath.

OLD HILL GIANT

The giant's so old, he's only got one fight left in him. And if he has his way, so do you.

Large 4th level troop [GIANT]
Initiative: +6

Really Gnarly Club +9 vs. AC—30 damage
   Miss that's a natural 6: Half damage (sometimes a miss is close enough)

R: Inaccurate Boulder Throw +8 vs PD—20 damage
   Inaccurate: After rolling the attack, pick two enemies and decide randomly which one is the actual target

Not the Giant He Used To Be: At the start of each of the giant's turns, pick a random player character. Through senility, blindness or some other complaint, the giant forgets that enemy exists. The giant will not attack that foe, and counts as being unaware of that foe for the purposes of sneak attacks.

AC	19	
PD	18	**HP 110**
MD	15	

ENCOUNTERS

As the adventurers wander through the hellhole, roll 1d12 for their next encounter. Add +1 to the roll for each previous encounter, and if you reroll the same encounter twice, move onto the next highest new encounter on the table (so, if you roll a 9 and you've already played through encounters 9 and 10, skip onto encounter 11).

Roll 1d12	Encounter
1–3:	Barren Land
4:	Fellow Travelers
5:	Burning Fog
6:	Flying Teeth
7:	Haunted Village
8:	Iconic Memories
9:	Bandit Camp
10:	Spacewarp
11:	Haunt Hounds (& Demonic Hunters)
12:	Fallen Wardstone
13:	The Miser's Cabin
14:	Firestorm
15:	Demon Fort
16+:	Center of the Hellhole

1–3: BARREN LAND

The foreboding landscape seems to swallow hope within its dark emptiness. Choose the adventurer with the lowest MD, deciding randomly in the case of ties. That adventurer picks up a dark passenger, a demonic spirit that masquerades as the adventurer's own shadow. At times, especially at night, it whispers in the adventurer's ear, pretending to be the voice of the character's own doubts and fears, and tells its host that all is lost and they will all perish in this hellhole. At other times, it detaches from the adventurer's shadow and commits petty acts of sabotage (cutting ropes, spoiling food, writing rude words in spellbooks, shaving beards) to sap the morale of the company.

Once discovered, the shadow flees. As it retreats, the adventurers make out its true shape—it's the shadow of a demon, sent to spy on the latest intruders. At some later point, pick a demon the player characters encounter and mention that they recognize the shape of its shadow.

4: FELLOW TRAVELERS

The adventurers encounter a pair of travelling traders, a dwarven potsmith named **Abkhaz** and a halfling cobbler named **Shana Lys.** The two accidentally wandered into the hellhole and are now lost and confused. Abkhaz has his hammer, but claims he hasn't used it in anger in years, and Shana has only a dagger. She does, however, have a set of dice with her; she's a gambler, and will challenge any willing player characters to a game of chance.

If questioned about why they were out on the moors, they are oddly defensive and evasive—"We got lost! We were on the road and got lost!). In fact, they were out on the moors burying a body. On the road, they met another traveler, a local farmer named **Hethwin**. Shana cheated in their dice game, he attacked her, and Abkhaz struck Hethwin with the hammer, killing him. Shana and Abkhaz blame each other for the crime.

To add to their misfortune, they buried Hethwin within the boundaries of the hellhole, and a freshly-murdered corpse is catnip to demons. He's been resurrected as a demonic wendigo spirit (*13th Age Bestiary*, p. 212) and is now spiraling through the hellhole, looking for his murderers.

5: BURNING FOG

By night, a horrible green fog rises from the ground. The fog smells like an accident in an alchemist's laboratory, and is caustic to the eyes and throat. It clings in an unwholesome way, collecting like greenish foam on the surface of objects that move through it. If the adventurers hurry through the fog, they end up caked in the gunk. It's unpleasant, but not dangerous.

Until dawn, that is. Direct exposure to sunlight causes the fog to explode into violent green flames that burn hot enough to melt metal. The fog clinging to the tops of the tors and hills ignites first, giving the player characters a few minutes' warning before the lowlands become a sea of fire and any fog-encrusted adventurers get incinerated. To survive, the adventurers need to either find a way to shield themselves from the sun, or else find shelter and wash off the fog before the sunlight reaches them. If the PCs ignore the threat, kill at least one of them.

6: FLYING TEETH

The adventures spot a flock of what appears to be strange white birds approaching from the center of Unending Woe. The flying creatures are very small, and seem more like insects in their movements than birds. As they draw closer, the nature of the things becomes clear.

They're teeth. Dozens of disembodied sets of sharp teeth, like giant-vampire fangs, chattering through the air. They circle above the adventurers, then dive down to attack. Roll for initiative.

The teeth fly in to attack in three waves, one wave per round. Roll initiative separately for each round, and if a wave has ten or more flying maws in it, break it up into at least two separate mobs, or three mobs if the wave has twenty or more mooks. The fact that the mooks are split up like this will probably be a factor, because targeting a maw that is the last of its mob won't be as effective as targeting newcomers . . . .

Skinless demon transformation: The table below lists the maximum number of skinless demons that should be added to the battle, one-at-a-time when a flying maw hits with its *transforming bite* attack. The fight is weighted to be a bit harder for large groups, who always seem to find a way to thwart diabolic plans.

You can go over the skinless demon limit if the PCs haven't suffered enough, but exceeding the limit by more than one risks a TPK.

If the maws roll badly, the fight may be easy. If the maws roll well and you hit the maximum number of skinless demons, the fight will feel more like a double-strength battle. You'll know how much credit to give the PCs!

FLYING MAW

These are proto-demons—minor chaotic spirits, who've gambled all their magic on growing teeth. This is their one shot at grabbing onto the material world and becoming actual demons.

2nd level mook [DEMON]
Initiative: +5

Transforming bite +6 vs. AC—4 damage
  Natural even hit: The flying maw becomes a skinless demon. The skinless demon acts on the same initiative as the flying maw it used to be.
  Transformations exceeded: If the fight has already reached its quota of skinless demons, deal +2 damage instead.

Flying: You know how disembodied flying monster teeth fly, right? Like angry bricks.

AC 17	
PD 16	HP 8 (mook)
MD 12	

Mook: Kill one flying maw mook for every 8 damage you deal to the mob.

SKINLESS DEMON

The thing that grows vein by vein out from the biting teeth that are still chewing on your shoulder looks like a skinned baboon with glowing green eyes and a spiky skull.

2nd level troop [DEMON]
Initiative: +5

Bite +7 vs. AC—7 damage

Jump in fangs first +7 vs. AC—10 damage
  Special: Usable only when the skinless demon starts its turn unengaged

AC 18	
PD 16	HP 32
MD 12	

#/Level of PCs	Flying Maw Wave 1	Flying Maw Wave 2	Flying Maw Wave 3	Max Skinless Demons
3 x 2nd level	2	2	2	3
4 x 2nd level	2	2	2	3
5 x 2nd level	2	2	2	3
6 x 2nd level	2	3	2	4
3 x 2nd level	3	3	3	3
4 x 3rd level	3	3	3	4
5 x 3rd level	3	3	3	5
6x 3rd level	3	3*	3	6

7: HAUNTED VILLAGE

There was once a village here called Lorgan's Croft, just a few huts huddled together in a sheltered spot by a brook. Lorgan's Croft had the misfortune to get caught in the hellhole. For weeks, the survivors debated what to do. Fleeing to the nearest town was impossible—what was supposed to be a journey of a few hours was now an infinite distance. Their only choices were to try to escape through the center of the hellhole, literally walking into the jaws of Hell, or else hunkering down and trying to defend their little hamlet against the demons that now walked the moors.

They decided to stay. They fortified their town, beat their ploughshares into swords, made the little chapel to the Gods of Light into a stronghold, and swore to fight side by side until the Empire came to save them.

The Empire never came. The demons could have overrun the villagers easily, but it was more fun to watch them tear themselves apart. As the months went by with no sign of rescue, and as their supplies ran out, the villagers turned on each other, destroying themselves more thoroughly than any demon could manage. Some fled to join the bandits serving **Caer Trenon** (Encounter 9); others set off for the hellhole's heart. Those who remained killed one another or went mad.

Searching the village reveals there's one survivor, a young girl named **Alyn.** Her family were among those who stayed, and they were attacked by neighbors who suspected they had food hidden in their hut. Afraid to travel deeper into the hellhole, Alyn now hides in the ruins of the village, scavenging for what little food remains.

The complication: A wandering vrock (*13th Age* core book, p. 211), drawn by the delightful aura of misery and murder in Lorgan's Croft, has also taken up residence in the village. Rescuing Alyn requires slaying the 6th level demon. If saved, Alyn can relate the sad tale of the village and hint that there is an exit through the center of the hellhole.

8: ICONIC MEMORIES

Pick a random icon from those represented among your player characters, or roll relationship dice and grab those 5s and 6s. If you have a lot of successful dice rolls, spread encounters out over the adventure. Some of these encounters are flashbacks; others might be framed as realizations on the part of the character. (If you're not confident about introducing unexpected plot twists like this, move this encounter to the start of the adventure, and replace it on the table with a wandering demon attack.)

 Archmage: A messenger-sprite sent by the Archmage reveals that the diviners at Horizon have detected unusual activity around the center of the hellhole. There seem to be a number of portals there, as opposed to the usual single gate to the Abyss. It might be a side effect of the hellhole's dimension-warping weirdness.

 **Crusader:** The adventurers find a fallen warrior bearing the badge of the Crusader. She's horribly warped and mutated, but it's clear that these changes weren't the cause of her death—her throat's been ripped out. She's one of the Crusader's Redeemed, warriors who were corrupted by demonic forces, but now fight to cleanse themselves through honorable death. She was likely a scout for the Crusaders' forces—perhaps they will soon march on Unending Woe. If you complete her mission, and bring intelligence back to the Crusader about the state of the hellhole's defenses, you will be justly rewarded.

 **Diabolist:** In the night, the adventure briefly senses an unfamiliar presence in the camp. There's a sudden warmth, and a lingering smell afterwards, the scent of roses and musk mixed with sulfur. A single, delicate footprint is found in the mud nearby, and next to it is something the adventurers need desperately—supplies, a map, a magical item, the smoking skull of a demon that's been hunting them...

 Dwarf King: The adventurers stumble on the remains of an old dwarf road. These paths were said to be made perfectly straight, aligned with the perfect geometry of the old dwarven empire. There might be some magic left in this road that will overcome the space-warping effects of the hellhole, if the players can do something dwarfy enough to make the stones remember.

 **Elf Queen:** On a hillside, the adventurers find a grove of trees sacred to the Elf Queen. This place is a sanctuary from the demons while the moon is in the sky. If the adventurers rest here, they each gain a bonus recovery until their next full heal-up.

 Emperor: Secretly, the Emperor entrusted you with a mission: you must secure a way out of this hellhole, and leave a trail for other unfortunate travelers to follow. It's not enough for you to merely escape. You must make sure that others can follow after you and get out the same way, and if that means bargaining with demons or forcing them to give safe passage to Imperial citizens, so be it. The Empire cannot yet close this hellhole, but it can make it less of a deathtrap.

 Great Gold Wyrm: By night, you are inspired by visions and dreams of the Wyrm's sacrifice. When you awake, you know that there are six portals at the heart of this hellhole. Five lead out, and one leads *down*. If that last portal is closed, the hellhole will be destroyed. Do you have the courage to follow the dragon and brave the fires of hell?

High Druid: This land is far from the reach of the current High Druid, but not from her predecessors. A previous High Druid lies buried beneath one of the tors. If the demons find his bones, they'll be able to use them as magical weapons against nature—your mission is to find these bones and burn them to ash, then scatter that ash on the wind. Of course, you'd never consider keeping any of the bones... even though they might be enough to buy you a way out of this hellhole.

 Lich King: That old beggar on the road— you don't know if he had one foot in the grave, or if he's already died and joined the King's followers. (You've seen such things before, undead who can still pass for living people. There are more of them than people suspect abroad in the Empire). With cold fingers, he pressed a scrap of paper into your hand. Is it a map of some part of this hellhole? If so, where does it lead?

 Orc Lord: You saw a few young half-orcs in the villages outside the hellhole. The Orc Lord's advance forces must not be too far away. If this hellhole were to vanish, or if a bargain struck with the demons, then the orcs could attack the Imperial forces on the far side of the high heath by surprise. Are you here to bring such a thing about, or thwart it?

 Priestess: Even in this gloomy and hopeless land, the light finds purchase. The Priestess' messenger told you before you came here that there was a hidden strength in this place, a hope concealed beneath sorrow and weariness. When you find it, the light will help you bring that strength to bear against the demons.

 Prince of Shadows: There was, remarked the stranger in the tavern, a man who once lived in the region now consumed by Unending Woe. He was once a rich merchant from Glitterhaegen, but grew to loathe the city and made a home in the country. He carried a fortune out of the city with him, and neither he nor his fortune has never been seen since. Perhaps his treasure still exists? Worth a look?

 The Three: The Black once hired a demonic assassin named Caer Trenon. She swindled the dragon, abandoned her mission and fled to this hellhole. Kill her and you shall be rewarded.

9: Bandit Camp

A small group of bandits make their lair in Unending Woe. Their leader, **Caer Trenon**, is a tiefling, and she's struck a bargain with the demons at the central fort. In exchange for letting her bandits leave the hellhole, she delivers a few victims as playthings for the demons. For Caer, it's win-win—the hellhole makes a virtually impregnable hideout, as no-one's willing to pursue her thieves into Unending Woe, and she gets to curry favor with the demons, making her more powerful. Most of her followers are ordinary humans, though, and they're terrified of both the demons and their increasingly insane leader. All the loot in the world is worth nothing if you're stuck outside in a hellhole.

The camp's located in a shallow cave network under one of the larger tors. It's hard to find unless you're a tracker (DC25) or know the secret signs used by allies of the Prince of Shadows. The bandits' reaction to the adventurers depends on how the party initially approach the cave. If they come in with swords drawn and combat spells blazing, go straight to a fight. If they approach as battle-hardened warriors lost in the hellhole, the bandits may offer them shelter and try to recruit them (hoping that maybe they'll be able to stop Caer Trenon.) If the bandits think the adventurers are just more desperate lost souls, it's ambush and looting time.

The demons' bargain was with Caer Trenon herself, not with the bandits. If the demons find out she's dead, they won't let the bandits escape through the portal.

Risk assessments: This fight is tough because Caer Trenon is tough and her *antipathy field* can make it unusually difficult for PCs to gang up on her.

CAER TRENON

Soon, she's going to stop thinking of the bandits as her followers and start categorizing them as her cattle. Red and gory are the appetites of demons, even half-demons.

Double-strength 3rd level wrecker [DEMON]
Initiative: +6

Wicked polearm +8 vs. AC (1 engaged or nearby enemy)—15 damage
Natural 16+: 5 ongoing damage (save ends)

Horned headbutt +8 vs PD—5 damage
Natural 16+: The target is dazed (save ends) and pops free of Caer Trenon
Limited use: Only usable when engaged by two or more enemies.
Special: Horned headbutt is a quick action.

R: Longbow +8 vs AC (two attacks)—10 damage

Antipathy field: While this creature is not engaged, each enemy attempting to move into engagement with her must succeed with a hard save (16+), using their level as a bonus to the roll. An enemy that fails stops their move near Caer Trenon, but not engaged with her, and takes 1d12 negative energy damage.

Reach tricks: Caer's weirdly extendable demon arms, her size, and the length of her polearm give her considerable reach in battle.

Nastier Specials
Mother of misfortune: If a creature attacking Caer Trenon with a melee attack rolls a natural 1-5, Caer Trenon may make a *horned headbutt* attack against that creature as a free action.

AC **19**	
PD **17**	**HP 99**
MD **15**	

BANDIT ARCHER

The best of a sorry lot. Well, the most durable, at least.

2nd level archer [HUMAN]
Initiative: +6

Shortsword +7 vs AC—7 damage

R: Bow +8 vs. AC—8 damage

Scamper: +4 bonus on disengage checks

AC **18**	
PD **15**	**HP 34**
MD **13**	

LOST BANDIT

The connection between murder, mayhem, robbery and greed and going to Hell isn't normally quite so clear-cut.

3rd level mook [HUMAN]
Initiative: +5

Sword, mace, spear or scavenged demon-bone club +8 vs AC—7 damage

R: Bow +7 vs. AC—6 damage

Desperate soul: Deals a critical hit with a natural attack roll of 19 or 20, but is eliminated from the battle if its attack roll is a natural 1 or 2.

AC **18**	
PD **17**	**HP 12 (mook)**
MD **11**	

Mook: Kill one lost bandit mook for every 12 damage you deal to the mob.

#/Level of PCs	Caer Trenon	Bandit Archer	Lost Bandit
3 x 2nd level	1	0	3
4 x 2nd level	1	1	3
5 x 2nd level	1	1	6
6 x 2nd level	1	2	6
3 x 2nd level	1	1	4
4 x 3rd level	1	2	6
5 x 3rd level	1	4	5
6 x 3rd level	1	6	8

10: SPACEWARP

The hellhole convulses, sending a ripple of space-warping weirdness through the heath. It looks like an expanding ring of distorted air as it rushes towards the adventurers. Assuming they don't have any clever defenses (like a ritual to shield them from the warp, or *teleporting* to the far side of the ring), roll 1d6 for each adventurer to see what happens to them.

1: **Twisted and Mangled:** Constitution check, DC25; fail and suffer 2d8 damage.

2: **Smashed:** As *twisted and mangled*, but the adventurer is also hurled into the air and comes down heavily, smashing one item of equipment. What's broken?

3: **Entombed:** As *twisted and mangled*, but when normality reasserts itself, the adventurer is partially entombed in the ground as space isn't put back together quite right, and one of the adventurer's limbs ends up overlapping with stone or earth. The adventurer takes 2d8 automatically and is stuck. Digging the trapped victim out safely takes several hours work; pulling the victim free by brute force inflicts another 2d8 damage.

4: **Dimensionally Flipped:** The adventurer doesn't come back quite right. In fact, he or she comes back *left*—the adventurer has been flipped around, and now speaks backwards, favors their other hand and so on. Until the next full heal-up, the adventurer cannot easily understand the speech or writing of unflipped individuals.

5: **Ethically Inverted:** Until the next full heal-up, the adventurer is replaced by their ethical inverse. Their attachments and friendships stay the same, but to anyone outside the player character group, they flip on the good/evil axis. A good character is evil, but still has the same friends and attachments, just complicated by being . . . nasty and unpleasant and shifty. A basically evil character is now basically good. Given that the PC are stuck in a nasty hellhole, this is meant as more of a roleplaying opportunity than a serious campaign problem!

6: **Distant Glimpse**: The weird distortions of space and time in the hellhole gives the adventurer a glimpse of a possible future. Roll 2d6 to see which encounter they glimpse.

11: HAUNT HOUNDS

The strange baying of demonic hounds echoes off the tors and cliffs! It sounds like dozens of demon dogs are in the area, but it's possible that the PCs might be able to evade a fight.

For dramatic purposes, you might want to tell the PCs that not much can be gained in this battle, it's a fight they may want to avoid. If they'd rather meet the problem head-on, or try and fail to avoid the battle, go to the Fight the Hounds section below.

If the PCs do manage to avoid fighting the hounds this time, this Haunt Hounds encounter is *not* removed from the encounter list like all the other encounters. Play out the encounter again the next time it is rolled.

Avoiding the hounds: A single PC of the players' choice makes a DC20 stealth or wilderness survival check. Increase the DC by 5 for each time the PCs have avoided the haunt hounds previously. An extremely cunning plan is worth a +2 bonus. Using an icon relationship advantage is worth a +5 bonus. Yes, the PC could burn an icon relationship advantage and still fail. Success with the roll means that the PCs evade the hounds, which bay off into the distance. As mentioned above, since the PCs avoided the haunt hounds, this encounter can happen again. The hounds have the PCs' scent and may be back.

Fight the hounds: In fact there aren't dozens of hounds on the PC's trail. Each demonic hound is possessed by as many as a dozen ghosts and bays like a chorus. If they catch up to the PCs, the haunt hounds attack until slain with no concern for their survival. They're tools of the demonic hunters who now step onto the trail of Encounter #11.

The haunt hounds' attacks may do some damage, but it's not a fight that's meant to threaten the PCs much. Not directly, in any case. It doesn't even count as a battle for purposes of determining when the PCs get a full rest.

Instead, the ghost within the haunt hounds may possess people they bite. These hauntings are set-up for when the demonic hunters catch up with their prey.

If you want to make the fight a bit more interesting, consider rolling initiative separately for each haunt hound in the fight.

After the battle, start mentioning that the PCs hear strange hunting horns out in the distance. If any of the heroes have been haunted by ghosts of the Heath, the ghosts cry out loud whenever they hear the horns, calling that the ones the hunters seek are "Here! They're here! We found them! Come this way!" The ghosts' cries have no appreciable effect, but it's going to be irritating at best and worrisome in truth.

Encounter #11 now shifts from the Haunt Hounds portion of the entertainment to the Demonic Hunters!

#/Level of PCs	Haunt Hounds
3 x 2nd level	2
4 x 2nd level	2*
5 x 2nd level	3
6 x 2nd level	4
3 x 2nd level	3
4 x 3rd level	4
5 x 3rd level	5
6 x 3rd level	6

*Increase the hounds' defenses and attack bonuses by 1.

HAUNT HOUND

Their howling is literally the tormented crying of lost souls. Slit a haunt hound's belly open, and you'll find a dozen half-digested ghosts coiling amidst ectoplasmic intestines.

2nd level spoiler [DEMON]
Initiative: +10

Bite +8 vs. AC—6 damage
> *Natural even hit:* Make a demonic haunting attack against the target or another nearby enemy as a free action
>> **C: Demonic haunting +6 vs. MD**—Target is haunted by 1d3 *ghosts of the Heath.*

Ghosts of the Heath: The spirits of the slain work for the demons now. Each ghost a PC is haunted by reduces the effect of any recoveries they use by hit points. At the end of each encounter, including this one, each haunted PC can attempt a separate hard save against each of the ghosts haunting them. If a save succeeds, that ghost fades away. If a save fails, the ghost stays with them. That's not good, and it could get very bad for any PC that is still haunted when the demonic hunters show up.

AC	17	
PD	12	**HP 34**
MD	16	

GAMEMASTER

The haunt hounds aren't that interesting if used as normal monsters. If you want to use them in other adventures, it's best to use them as set-up for a stronger foe the PCs will encounter later.

For roleplaying fun in this adventure, create names and personalities for each of the ghosts, or ask the players to help. Depending on the ghosts' personalities, one or two of them might be susceptible to being dealt with by icon relationship advantages.

11 (PART TWO): DEMONIC HUNTERS

The hunters won't show up until after the PCs have fought the haunt hounds. The hunters' weird horns will start in the distance, growing ever-closer, so for a change, PCs who want to cast spells or use other abilities to prepare for battle will have ample opportunity. That's good, because this is a double-strength fight.

DEMONIC HUNTER

They ride steeds made of stitched-together bits of human and animal corpses, and carry swords made of thorn and bones. You really don't want to look too closely at their musical instruments, by the way.

4th level wrecker [DEMON]
Initiative: +10

Slashing sword +9 vs. AC—13 damage
> *Natural 16+:* The demon may pop free of the target and continue moving, if it wishes.

R: Hunting bow +8 vs. AC (1 nearby or far away enemy)—12 damage

Haunt slayer: Add the number of *ghosts of the heath* haunting a target of the demonic hunters' attacks as both an attack bonus and a damage bonus.

Sound the horn: As a quick action, one demonic huntsman can sound its horn each round. A random PC who is being haunted by one or more *ghosts of the heath* must roll a normal save (11+). If the save fails, that PC is hampered until the end of its next turn.

AC	20	
PD	16	**HP 52**
MD	16	

#/Level of PCs	Demonic Hunters	Haunt Hounds
3 x 2nd level	2	2
4 x 2nd level	3	2
5 x 2nd level	4	2
6 x 2nd level	5	3
3 x 2nd level	3	2
4 x 3rd level	4	3
5 x 3rd level	6	2
6 x 3rd level	7	3

PERILS

Upslides: Landslides are dangerous enough, but upslides have another downside—on a 16+, the victim is flung high into the air. With luck, that's only another 2d6 damage. Otherwise, you land somewhere more unpleasant like an invisible eagle nest or a demon midden, or get hurled off the mountain entirely.

Belligerent Words: Terribly angry, belligerent or rude phrases stomp through the mental landscape of the mountain, looking for mouths to give voice to them. A character hit by this "peril" has an outburst once per encounter where they are unable to contain their frustration with some aspect of their situation. In a combat, you can usually get away with complaining about one of your enemies. In a non-combat encounter, though, it's more likely to be the habits or behaviours of your fellow adventurers that get your goat. Occasionally, you'll shout in the forgotten tongue once spoken in Bar-en-Huil. After such an outburst, make a save (11+, or 16+ if the GM is having fun tormenting you) to escape the curse.

LOCATIONS

CLAW'S CAVE

Lord Claw rules his shrunken domain from a cave network lined with the bones of lesser demons who rebelled against his reign. They're not quite dead—a slain demon is usually banished and returned to the Abyss, but a horribly mangled, crippled, mostly-

dead demon makes a stunning wall ornament pour encourager les autres. Those lost in the worm-tunnels running off from the main cave can hear the bones creak and whisper to one another.

To maintain his control over the other demons, Lord Claw forbids them from gathering. He's divided his followers into several packs, and one pack may not speak, fight or consort with another pack without his express permission. This may be a boon for adventurers delving the dungeon, as they can fight one pack of demons without worrying about reinforcements showing up—indeed, one pack of demons may cheer from the sidelines and give supportive advice while the adventures fight their way through another rival pack.

The definite traitor: One imp, named Barygos, may attempt to take advantage of such distractions to propose an alliance aimed at taking out the chief. See Barygos' stats below.

The strongpoint: Claw's own lair is the deepest part of the cave. Here, on the edge of the gate, he tries increasingly desperate and messy rituals to hold the gate open and preserve his domain, hoping to dominate reality the same way he dominates his other demons.

DENIZENS

The demons encountered as Lord Claw's followers are mostly low level demons. The new demon types appearing on pages 43-45 work perfectly if you'd like to add something the PCs may have not fought before. We're not going to duplicate those stats here, in Claw's Peak you can build your own battles.

When Claw Peak demons have random demon abilities, use the new table on page 43 or the following table that's customized to Claw Peak.

RANDOM CLAW PEAK DEMON POWERS (D4 FOR LESSER DEMONS, D6 FOR NASTIER ONES)

1: *Rockslider*—whenever the demon moves to engage a new foe, the demon deals an extra 2d4 damage if it hits with its first attack

2: *Giant claws*—increase the demon's basic melee damage by +3

3: *Teleport 1d3 times each battle*

4: *Angry*—while the demon is staggered, it may add the escalation die's value to its attack rolls

5: *Demonic speed*—the demon can take an extra action while the escalation die is 4+

6: *Eagle summoner*—once per battle, every creature engaged with the demon takes 2d4 ongoing damage (normal save ends) from invisible demon eagle allies. Then demon the pops free and gains flight for the rest of its turn.

LORD CLAW

Better to rule in a hole than serve in Hell.

Large 4th level leader [demon]
Initiative: +9

Giant Claw +9 vs. AC—25 damage
Natural even hit: Lord Claw can grab the target as long as he isn't already grabbing a creature. The grabbed foe cannot move except to teleport, pop free, or attempt to disengage, and disengage attempts take a −5 penalty unless the creature hit Lord Claw with an attack this turn.
Natural odd hit: Lord Claw flings the target away, popping the target free and dealing another 2d6 damage.

[special trigger] **Squeeze +13 vs. PD**—30 damage. Lord Claw can only make a squeeze attack against a grabbed foe.

C: Hellspit +8 vs. PD (1d3 nearby enemies)—15 fire damage
Natural 16+: Have 5 ongoing fire damage, too (save ends)

Shout at Underlings: At the start of each of Lord Claw's turns, roll a d6 and consult the table below.
1: *Incoherent rage-filled ramblings*: No effect
2: *Stop dying, idiot!:* One nearby demon ally may immediately save against an ongoing effect
3: *Get them!:* One nearby demon ally may immediately take a free move action.
4: *Hit them!:* One nearby demon ally may immediately make a free basic attack.
5: *Reinforcements:* Add 1d4 dretch mooks (*13th Age*, p. 210) to the battle. They have the same initiative score as Lord Claw, acting immediately after him.
6: *Listen, all of you!:* Roll again on the table using a d4, but the effect extends to all nearby demons.

Nastier Specials
Not Going Back: Lord Claw continue to fight when reduced to 0 or fewer hit points. He must make a save at the start of every turn to keep fighting. If he fails, he dies. If he succeeds, he may act normally, and may add the value of the escalation die to his attacks.

AC	20	
PD	18	**HP 108**
MD	14	

BRINGING OUT THE DRETCH

Since part of the fun you've had as GM reading this section is the knowledge that Lord Claw is 'actually' a dretch, how can you make that part of the fun for the PCs? For a change we're not providing any answers. Maybe you'll come up with something and tell us what you did!

BARYGOS THE WORM

"Hi, I'm Barygos. I'm a nimp. Sorry, AN imp. Anyway, want to team up, overthrow Claw and rule this hellhole as dashing adventurer and freakish scalded-baby-with-wings-and-fangs sidekick?"

4th level spoiler [DEMON]
Initiative: +9

Festering Claws +9 vs. AC—8 damage, and 5 ongoing damage

R: Blight Jet +8 vs. PD—10 damage and the target is dazed (save ends)
Natural 16+: If the target is nearby, Barygos takes cover behind the target; attacks on Barygos by the target's allies suffer a −4 attack penalty as long as the target remains dazed.

Curse Aura: Whenever a creature attacks Barygos and rolls a natural 1-5, that creature takes 1d10 psychic damage.

Curse Mastery: As a quick action, Barygos can redirect any nearby curse to any nearby target. This includes psychic damage from his *curse aura*, free-floating curses like the *belligerent words* (p. 62), the effects of a tiefling's *curse of chaos*, a hag's death curse, a demonologist's curse spells, and anything else that the GM thinks sounds like a curse. Adventurer-tier only, or maybe a champion-tier effect if Barygos tries really hard and succeeds with a hard save.

Clumsy Flight: One of Barygos' wings was cut off by Lord Claw. He can still fly, but only for short distances and it's very tiring. He'll whine about this at length if you let him.

AC	21	
PD	14	**HP 55**
MD	19	

TREASURES OF CLAW PEAK

Death-Staff of Bar-en-Huil: Once per day, when casting a ritual, gain a +5 bonus to your skill check. Your description of the ritual must explain how calling on the ghosts of the former inhabitants of Bar-en-Huil helps you accomplish the task. Unless you're someone very unique, the ghosts are never happy to serve you. *Quirk:* Find it hard to breathe when scared or stressed.

FLOATING MARKET

Location: Eastern Hellmarsh
Level Range: Any

The Floating Market is sometimes the largest town in the Hell Marsh. It's a huge raft of weed-bound mud, woven reeds, small boats, salvaged junk and demonic flowstone, breaking apart and reforming in a constant chaos.

Although it's a hellhole—there's a gate to hell somewhere in the town's marshy underbelly—most of the population are humanoids. The Floating Market is a trade town, like Nomad (*13th Age*, p. 274). The Diabolist keeps the peace here by means of a system of special favors. When you enter the Floating Market, you get to draw a knucklebone token from a basket. Most of the knucklebones are bone-white, but a small number are painted black. If you've got a black token, then if someone cheat or threatens you, you can bring a case before the Diabolist and her magistrates. Guilt is certain; punishments are harsh and imaginative.

As no-one knows who's currently got a black token and who doesn't, committing any crime in the town is risky. There's a fierce trade in tokens—a demon might take the law into its own claws and intercede in a street mugging in the hopes that the victim of the mugging is carrying a token, and could be induced to trade that token in exchange for the demon's rough justice. Over time, unused black tokens find their way to the demon lords, merchant princes and demonologists who rule the Floating Market; eventually, one of them will cash in a mountain of black tokens to bring down some rival.

As the geography of the market keeps changing, the locals have adopted the directions 'uphell' and 'downhell', meaning away from or towards the town's hellhole. As only demons and long-term residents can instinctively sense the proximity of the portal, the main use of this convention is to bewilder and test visitors to the Market.

GAMEMASTER

The Floating Market works best in campaigns where you've got a player-character demonologist or two, or at least want to emphasize demons. It's the equivalent of Horizon for infernal magic, although it also treads on the toes of Shadowport (as a den of scum and villainy) and Drakkenhall (as a city of monsters). Use it if you want to keep the Citadel of the Diabolist (p. 100) in reserve for later tiers.

In a campaign where demons aren't the focus, or where hellhole encounters are all about demon-slaying, you may not need the Floating Market. If so, feel free to sink it and send its denizens into the territories you are concerned with.

UNUSUAL BUSINESSES OF THE FLOATING MARKET

1: **Flesh-Flensing Chirugeons**, for demons that dislike their form, and want to reincarnate as something more fetching)
2: **Sacred Crocodile Scrimshaw Artists,** for blasphemies you can hang on your wall.
3: **Whimsicologists**, who—for a hefty fee—predict the Diabolist's moods and suggest the best time to approach her
4: **Swamp Guides Who Won't Murder You And Leave You To Die.** Seriously, that's what it says on their sign.
5: **Enemy-on-a-Stick Snack Stand**—because who doesn't want to eat a small squirming meat homunculus that looks just like your worst enemy? Chicken or beef flavour.
6: **Casino of Black and White.** The black tokens let you call on the Diabolist to enforce 'justice'. No-one's quite sure what the white ones do, so what's the harm in gambling them?
7: **Tyrant in a Well.** Converse with the shades of some of the most infamous, monstrous and rightfully damned tyrants in history by shouting down a well that extends all the way to Hell. Patrons are warned not to stick their heads down too far, as possession by a legendary tyrant often offends.
8: **Demon Post.** Demons cannot leave their hellholes, so the only reliable way to ship goods between one hellhole and another is to go through the post. It's just like guarding a caravan, if the caravan was full of screaming souls and unwholesome things.
9: **Dragonpie Shop.** Does not contain actual dragon—it's mostly eel. Mostly. Each dragonpie is baked with a small effigy of the Great Gold Wyrm hidden somewhere inside it. It's considered unlucky to be served the slice containing the worm, and a statistically significant number of demon lords have choked to death on golden effigies. Everyone else thinks this is hilarious.
10: **Soul Value Assayers,** who'll work out the market price of your soul and suggest the best time to sell it.
11: **House of Unwelcome Truths:** The demons here can answer almost any question by consulting their endless piles of scrolls and notes. The catch is that to enter, you must entrust to them your most cherished or shameful secret.
12: **No-Questions-Asked Leatherworking & Tannery**
13: **Eyeball Emporium.** Services include demon grafts, visions of what an eyeball observed in the last few minutes of life, magic talismans, and these delicious sugar-frosted snacks made from used eyeballs.

DISTRICTS

The districts of the Floating Market are called wards, which is either a bad pun or a covert reference to the magical protections set in place to keep the demons from killing each other. The layout of the town changes regularly, so it's pointless saying that, say, the Fisher's Ward is next to the Bazaar Infernal, except as a momentary likelihood.

When the hellhole first formed, an especially powerful demon, a crocodile-headed vrock of prodigious appetites,

declared herself the Demon Queen of the Floating Market. She was promptly ritually dismembered and dissected by emissaries of the Diabolist. She's still alive, but her various organs are stored in life-support jars. These jars are symbols of authority in the Floating Market—if you've got one, it's a sign that the Diabolist (and therefore, everyone else) considers you the boss of that particular ward.

Fisher's Ward

Run by humans and other non-demons, Fisher's Ward resembles any of the other marsh villages in the region. Small wooden houses with jetties or verandas hang over the water, connected to one another by rope-bridge walkways. Hundreds of fishing lines and nets drag in the water, and little canoes dart in and out of the waterways like flies around a corpse. Oppression and exploitation are rife in the Fisher's Yard—naïve young people drawn to the Market in the hopes of making their fortune or selling their souls for some extravagant dream get caught in the nets here and end up as indentured servants or worse.

Down the alleys of the Fisher's Ward are the demon-blood dens, where addicts smoke herbs that grow only in hellholes and experience vivid visions of the hells below. No thrill is as desirable as the moment when you wake up from a demons-blood bender and realize that you're not in hell. Conversely, no vice is as likely to land you in hell as smoking demons-blood. All the demons-blood dens are ultimately under the control of **Pyar the Ferryman**, a fat tiefling who travels through Fisher's Ward on a palanquin borne by enchanted orangutans.

The cheapest inns in the city are in the Fisher's Ward, like *The Red Flower* or the *Crusader's Rest*. The biggest inn, *The Market Tavern*, mysteriously fell into the swamp a few weeks ago and was left behind as the Floating Market continued on its course. Eyewitnesses insist there were still a few survivors, clinging to the wreckage, but no doubt the crocodiles got 'em by now.

The boss of the ward is **Old Nann**, who runs a soup kitchen in the lower ward. Whether she's got an arrangement with Pyar, or if Nann's powerful enough in her own right to run the ward is a secret known only to her. Once a year, on a certain feast-day, Old Nann pops the canopic jar open and adds a few scraps of vrock liver to the fish stew, giving those who eat at her table the power to fly for a few hours.

The Bazaar Infernal

The Bazaar is why most people come to the Floating Market. It's a warren of narrow alleyways, tents, booths and peddlers selling their goods on the walkways or from little boats that punt from canal to canal. Most of the goods for sale here came up from hell, so it's the place to buy demon-forged armor, weird arcane supplies, bottled demons and other weird curios, as well as traffic with demons and make unholy deals. More souls are sold and more dark bargains struck in the coffeeshops of the bazaar than anywhere else in the Empire.

The bazaar is under the special protection of the Diabolist. Her agent here, and master of the ward, is **Generosity**. He—it?—wears a flowing purple robe that hides his body completely, and a golden face-mask depicting a shining sun. Generosity moves through the crowds like a smiling giant, handing out black and white tokens to passersby. Sometimes, he gives out little scraps of paper with advice or instructions on them. It is unwise to ignore a note from Generosity.

More than the rest of the town, the market is ever-changing. There are far more temporary traders and pop-up booths than there are permanent establishments. Of the latter, the two that have endured the longest are the *Café Diabolique*, operated by the **Bugwort** clan of halflings, famed for their discretion, and *Arcanum of Unknown Delights*, run as it has been for centuries by a hag who calls herself **Yiska of the Tooth.**

Ward of Thrashing Limbs

Only demons and the deaf live in this ward. Here, uncounted thousands of limbs sprout from the muddy ground of the floating island. The limbs are of all shapes and sizes, from all sorts of donors. Human arms, demon claws, dragon's tails, giant- and dwarf-sized legs, salvage from golems and tentacles from weird monsters, all flailing wildly. The ones on the underside of the raft move in unison enough to swim, pushing the raft—and hence, all of the Floating Market—through the swamp.

In the middle of the island is the Drummer's Tower, where bands of drummers beat on drums of human skin to keep the limbs moving in time. The town's master of drums is an orc called **Magger**. He fled the Orc Lord's armies, and bears the brand of a coward upon his back.

Few people dwell in this part of the town, but overcrowding has forced some to try living here. The usual solution is either to hack away limbs to clear space (they regrow like weeds, so you need to keep chopping or you'll have hands coming up through your floorboards) or just tie a platform between four tall limbs and get used to your house waving this way and that. Parts of the ward are used for storage and warehousing. In fact, an enterprising sorceress called **Fireeyes** has established herself as the ruler of the town docks—through strategic *shocking grasps*, she can cause some of the larger topside limbs to bend at her whim, allowing her to use them as cranes for unloading cargo.

Old Ganet

Back before there was a hellhole here, this was a marsh village. Now, it's the oldest district in the impossible town that's grown up around it. Ganet's inhabited by demons and tieflings; the district's on the cusp of slipping into hell, and reality is noticeably mushy in this part of town. If you can cope with screaming faces materializing on the walls, or gravity being optional, or sudden bursts of colorless fire like rainstorms, then you can try living in Old Ganet.

The skyline of the district is dominated by the Keep of Chains, a fortress of black stone. It could only stand in this ward—if the building were anywhere else in town, it would sink instantly. From his perch, **Lord Bonecracker** commands the town's defenses; he's a vrock demon, possibly a reincarnation of the former demon queen. Old Ganet also contains the Diabolist's court, where she or her emissaries pass sentence on those brought before her by means of the black tokens.

Boats full of would-be apprentices and cultists depart from Old Ganet once a month, heading deeper into the swamp. Allegedly, these boats are bound for the Diabolist's secret citadel.

THOUSAND-TOWERS ISLE

The thousand towers are tottering and fragile, and sway alarmingly when the wind blows through the swamps. Of course there aren't *really* a thousand towers, but it's hard to get an accurate count as new towers spring up to replace those that fall over. The towers are inhabited by spellcasters—demonologists, infernal sorcerers, renegade clerics, heretic wizards, burning necromancers, even hellish druids—who are drawn to the Floating Market in search of secrets and arcane power. Familiars and imps flit around the tower-tops. The lower parts of the ward are a cesspool of alchemical run-off and botched summoning attempts. Every so often, flocks of vrocks descend and carry off great wedges lopped out of the upper towers; no-one's sure if the inhabitants of those towers are being taken to the Diabolist for further education, or if they've transgressed some secret law and so doomed themselves.

The master of this ward is determined by an annual arcane contest! Last year's winner turned up dead in an alleyway, stabbed by an anti-magic dagger, so her place was taken by the runner-up, the tiefling demonologist **Nine Moons Falling.** She's convinced that someone's after the vrock brain-in-a-jar she holds, and is looking for some patsy to take the relic and the ward off her hands so she can get back to her studies in ending the world.

THE REDWAY

The Redway is *the* demon district. No rustic marsh architecture of mud-and-reed houses here—Redway's style can be summarized as 'butchery and blood', with buildings carved out of demon flesh or just straight-up piles of skulls. Visitors aren't welcome—if you want to deal with demons, go to the bazaar and don't trouble them at home. Violence in the Redway rarely spills out into the rest of town, but all the black tokens in the world won't protect you if you wander far into this ward—which you'll probably have to do if you're looking for a specific demon, especially a craftsman or mercenary warlord.

The toughest demon in the Redway is **Ahr'gh'hul,** who broke free of the Crusader's chains and now plots ways to sabotage and defeat the Crusader. Yeah, that's a One Unique Thing for a monster boss! Anyone who feeds his dreams of vengeance can gain an audience with the brutal boss. Stats not included, so if the PCs decide to make a fight of it, take this demon *all* the way up and reintroduce the "PCs can always flee" rules.

MOONPOOL

The moonpool is the town's pleasure district, a narrow ring of low buildings around a pool of unnaturally clear water. Sacred crocodiles—it's seriously bad luck to kill them—swim majestically between the little boats and under the late-night bars around the Moonpool.

There's a temple to one of the Gods of Light in the Moonpool, and the high priestess of that temple is **Hayla Silvershon.** It's one of the Diabolist's little jokes to let a temple dedicated to healing and tranquility survive in a city of corruption and vice. The ward boss, a silent marilith called the **Eightfold Glaive,** is under strict orders not to interfere with the operations of the temple, making it a sanctuary for outsiders in the Floating Market. When the moon is full, the moonpool's waters turn silver with holy power, and no demon can abide their touch.

THE FLOATING MARKET & THE ICONS

We're leaving a couple of the icons out of this list. The Lich King and the High Druid don't seem to have strong interests near the Floating Market. Your PCs might change that. But many of the other icons already care, or could be made to care.

 The **Diabolist** first—She probably uses the Floating Market for many of her dealings with the outside world. Or if she doesn't, she *pretends* to, in order to get her real business done elsewhere.

 Maybe the **Archmage** turns a blind eye to the Floating Market—it's outside his wards and outside his purview. Or perhaps there are arcane materials his agents can obtain in the Floating Market that can't be found anywhere else. Maybe agents of the Archmage occasionally remind the Diabolist that she needs to keep the Floating Market under control, or else. Maybe the Crusader would love to discover proof of this collaboration.

 The **Crusader,** unsurprisingly, wants to destroy the Floating Market. But it's too deep inside the Diabolist's domain and too, well, floaty for his standard methods. If the Crusader has sent an army towards the Floating Market at some point in the past, that army probably got so mired and misled that no one wants to acknowledge its existence. Maybe there's plunder to be found where the army fell apart?

 The Floating Market is a den of thieves right on the **Dwarf King's** south-western border, and he hates thieves. If the Market ever leaves the swamp and floats down Torin's Glory, the forts along the northern shore have standing orders to bombard it with catapults.

 The **Elf Queen** has many spies in the Market. The same could be said of the Floating Market's spies in the Court of Stars . . . .

The **Emperor** dislikes the Floating Market, and has in the past made attempts to destroy it. Now, he has more pressing issues, with the Orc Lord advancing from the north. Some of the Emperor's advisers suggest allying with the folk of Hell Marsh and the barbarian tribes and sorcerers of Moonwreck. Both regions were once part of the Empire; what if the people living in those lands were made Imperial citizens in exchange for their support in battling the Orc Lord? In such a scenario, could the Floating Market be raised to the status of an imperial city? Would that be final proof of the Emperor's depravity? Or a sign that he's willing to risk everything to save the Empire?

The **Great Gold Wyrm** threw himself into hell to stop demons from destroying the world. If he ever saw the Floating Market, he might question if his sacrifice was worth it. There's a saying in the north: "like a paladin at the Floating Market," and it refers to the rarest of problems.

The **Priestess** dreams of the Moon Temple; specifically, she has prophetic dreams of it burning, and intends to avert this fate.

The **Prince of Shadows** actually runs this town. Smugglers bring hellish goods and other treasures down Torin's Glory and Calamity, then across the Bitterwood to Shadow Port. Or that's what the smugglers who want your help are sure of.

The **Three** see Drakkenhall mirrored in the Floating Market, and have considered stealing it. The hellhole travels with the Market, after all, and so there's no reason why the Market couldn't be anchored off Drakkenhall while retaining profitable commercial ties with Hell.

DENIZENS

The Floating Market is a stable and safe hellhole. Yes, there are sacred crocodiles blessed by dead gods cruising through the marsh, there's the occasional belch of sulfurous gas, and there's every chance you'll be eaten in your sleep by demon bedbugs if nothing else, but this town won't kill you by accident.

On the other hand, the monsters appearing below would be willing to kill you on purpose if you go looking for a fight.

RANDOM FLOATING MARKET DEMON POWERS (d4 FOR LESSER DEMONS, d6 FOR BIGGER ONES)

1: *Water Walking*—the demon can walk on water as though it was solid ground

2: *Resist Fire 18+*

3: *Thief*—the demon becomes *invisible* whenever the escalation die is even.

4: *Resist energy 12+*

5: *Black Token*—this demon has a black token which it threatens to use when it first becomes staggered. Continue to attack this demon, and you'll incur the wrath of the Diabolist.

6: *Call allies*—once per battle as a standard action, the demon can call for aid. Another demon joins the fight (usually two levels lower than the one who summoned it)

FLESH-CARVER

Demonic butchers and surgeons. Six arms, so they can cut you open, remove a few unnecessary organs, and sew you back up again all at the same time. Big, toothy mouths with long tongues behind their veils, to make sure no flesh or spilled blood goes to waste...

5th level spoiler [DEMON]
Initiative: +9

Unnecessary scalpel +10 vs. AC—10 damage
Natural even hit: The demon may immediately make a free *unnecessary surgery* attack.
Natural odd hit: 5 ongoing damage (save ends)

[special trigger] **Unnecessary surgery +10 vs. PD**—6 damage
Natural even hit: Roll on the *hideous grafts* table, and the demon may immediately make a free *unnecessary sutures* attack.
Natural odd hit: 5 ongoing damage (save ends)

[special trigger] **Unnecessary sutures +10 vs. MD**—6 damage
Natural even hit: The target is vulnerable until the end of its next turn.
Natural odd hit: 5 ongoing damage (save ends)

Hideous grafts: The demon's impromptu surgery has an odd effect...

1: The patient may immediately heal using a free recovery, but demonic flesh grows to cover any healed wounds.

2: The patient's evil hand makes an immediate basic attack on a nearby ally.

3: The patient suffers terrible stomach cramps, and is weakened until the end of its next turn.

4: The flesh-eating worm eggs hatch prematurely. 5 ongoing damage (save ends).

5: The patient takes another 2d6 damage. If still alive, roll on the Random Demon Abilities table of the GM's choice.

6: The patient takes another 3d6 damage. If still alive, permanently gain a magic item in the form of a demonic claw, eye or other body part surgically transplanted to the victim.

R: Evaluate the patient +10 vs MD (one nearby or far away enemy)—10 damage, and for the rest of the encounter, the demon may choose to subtract one from its natural attack rolls when attacking the target.

Nastier Specials

C: Hurl noxious flasks +9 vs PD (1d4 nearby enemies in a group)—14 acid damage, and 5 ongoing acid damage
Limited use: 1/battle

AC	22	
PD	15	**HP 80**
MD	19	

Demons' Allies

Flesh-carver demons hang around with a variety of low-lives, including greater claw demons (page 45), despoiler mages who help trick creatures into signing consent forms, and undead like zombies that didn't quite survive the surgical process.

Demon of the dice could hang out with most any demons, but our best money is on cambion assassins (*13th Age Bestiary*, page 30). That could be the PCs' second or third sign that someone wants them dead, and is setting odds.

Demon of the Dice

Care to try your luck? These demonic gamblers lurk in the casinos and backstreets of the Floating Market. Invariably, they're followed by a swarm of dicethralls, desperate shades hoping for one last chance to win back their stake.

6th level caster [DEMON]
Initiative: +12

Green claw +11 vs. AC—20 damage
Natural miss: Double or nothing? The demon's target may choose to let the demon make an immediate free *green claw* attack. If the target agrees, and the demon misses again, the demon may not attack that target again for the rest of the battle unless all targets have won the double or nothing bet with the demon, in which case the wager resets and everyone is a legal target until they once again win the bet.

[special trigger] **Painbolt +11 vs MD**—15 psychic damage
Miss: 5 ongoing psychic damage.

Wager: At the start of a combat, the demon of the dice may wager on any one enemy. When that enemy scores a crit or reduces a foe to 0 hit points, the demon of the dice may immediately make a free *painbolt* attack on any target *other* than the subject of the wager.

Nastier Specials

Unlucky number: At the start of each round, the Gamemaster rolls a d20 and notes the result. Whenever a creature (ally or enemy) rolls that number, the demon of the dice *must* make a free *painbolt* attack on that target.

AC	22	
PD	16	**HP 100**
MD	20	

Dicethrall

It's hard to tell if these grey shades are ghosts, or demons, or living wretches. Maybe all three are present, their distinctions lost in the common madness of their addiction. The dice don't play favorites.

6th level mook [DEMON]
Initiative: +10

Desperate slap +11 vs. AC—12 damage

Luckthieves: If an enemy that the dicethrall is engaged with rolls a natural 20, that creature becomes vulnerable to the dicethralls for the rest of the combat.

AC	21	
PD	21	**HP 23**
MD	16	

Mook: Kill one dicethrall mook for every 23 damage you deal to the mob.

RED CRAG CASTLE

Location: Anywhere in or near the Empire
Level Range: Champion tier (5-6)

You can see Red Crag Castle for miles around. The crag rises like a scar from the flat lands around, commanding a view over all the approaches. The castle itself is a greyish growth running the length of the crag's spine. From a distance, it appears to have been built without any coherent plan, an unlikely mess of walls, towers, keeps and buttresses.

The castle had an evil reputation even before it became a hellhole. The Vocnort family ruled here, and they were possessed of unusual tastes and questionable loyalties. They were allies, the stories say, of the Diabolist, suggesting that this hellhole is the result of some arcane accident or divine justice. However it happened, the castle was overrun with demons when the hellhole opened, and virtually all the Vocnorts were slain.

Red Crag Castle is now a nightmarish dungeon infested with hundreds of demons. The corridors are killing grounds now; the towers are both tombs and slaughterhouses. Four powerful demons war for control of the Crag, and it appears to be a stalemate between their forces. The surviving Vocnorts may be the deciding factor in the demons' war, as only members of that accursed family know all the secrets and blood-magic wards of the castle . . . .

FACTIONS

The heart of this hellhole is a split into four: four factions of demons vie for control and two groups of mostly-humans seek vengeance or compensation.

For the demons of Red Crag, use the following random demon powers. The two results that refer to faction powers are explained in each of the faction write-ups below. If you've introduced a demon that has no faction, use the table on page 43 instead.

RANDOM RED CRAG DEMON ABILITIES (D4 FOR LESSER DEMONS, D6 FOR GREATER DEMONS)

1: *Deathwish*—The demon takes a –2 penalty to all defenses and gains a +3 attack bonus.
2: *Entropic warp*—When an enemy deals miss damage to the demon, that enemy also takes half that amount of damage.
3: *Faction ability 1*—Determined by the demon's faction in Red Crag Castle.
4: *Big hate*—Each battle, the demon gains a +4 attack bonus until the end of the battle against the first enemy that hits it with an attack.
5: *Faction ability 2*—Determined by the demon's faction in Red Crag Castle.
6: *Demonic speed*—The demon can take an extra action each turn while the escalation die is 4+.

BARON STEEL'S BRIGADE

Baron Steel considers himself to be the ruler of the hellhole. He has crowned himself with a steel circlet adorned with the eyes of every Vocnort he could catch as a token of his authority. He's a disciplined, militaristic demon of the balor line. He's not a full-strength balor, but give him another few decades and he'll shuck his heavy armor and flame on. Baron Steel commands a cadre of like-minded demonic shock troops. His forces control the Great Keep and Library Tower of Red Crag.

The Brigade has an uneasy alliance with the Chiding Ladies, predicated on safe passage to the Library Tower. Steel hates the Rockgrubs and has embarked on a long campaign to wipe them out. If he could, he would ally with or wipe out the Revelers, too, but they are a less pressing threat than the Grubs and frustratingly chaotic to deal with.

Demonologists beware: Of all the factions, Baron Steel's Brigade will be the worst disposed towards a player character who turns out to be a demonologist, or for that matter, any demon summoner. Steel feels that the balance of power is tilting in his favor and assumes newly summoned demons might slant things the wrong way. Ironically, given that Steel is potentially a balor, he'd be more likely to accept a slaughter path devotee as an ally, since they seem likely to share the same aesthetic.

Most likely to melee: If you're invading Red Crag Castle and you don't end up fighting Baron Steel's Brigade, you're either very lucky, very stealthy, or a good friend of militant demons. To that end, we're providing more monster stats for members of the Brigade than the other factions in the hellhole, including a couple lower level versions of higher-powered demons. To supplement the members of the Brigade statted up below, consider using cambion katars (*13th Age Bestiary*, page 31).

BARON STEEL'S BRIGADE FACTION ABILITIES

Use these when the Red Crag Castle Random Demon Abilities table yields a faction ability.

*Faction Ability 1—***Militant:** Gain a +2AC bonus when fighting next to at least two other demons of this faction.

*Faction Ability 2—***Squad Leader:** When this demon rolls a natural even miss, one nearby allied mook may immediately make a free basic attack.

SKIANZOU (KNIFE DEMON)

The followers of Baron Steel jangle as they swagger. Every one of them has at least half-a-dozen blades rammed through its body like some ghastly pincushion of doom.

6nd level troop [DEMON]
Initiative: +11

Sword +13 vs. AC—14 damage
  Natural even hit: The skianzou may immediately make a *body of knives* attack as a free action.
  Natural odd hit: The target is vulnerable to the attacks of demons until the end of its next turn.

[[*special trigger only*]] **Body of knives +13 vs. AC**—10 ongoing damage.

R: Hurled blade +13 vs. AC—25 damage
  Natural odd: The skianzou takes 5 damage.

Nastier Specials
Swordcatcher: If an attacker using a melee weapon rolls a natural 1-5 when attacking a skianzou, the skianzou may choose to allow that attack to count as a hit instead. The skianzou takes half damage from this attack, and absorbs the attacker's weapon into its body. The weapon can only be retrieved when the skianzou is destroyed.

AC	22	
PD	20	**HP 90**
MD	16	

LESSER HOOKED DEMON

Alive and screaming.

6th level mook [DEMON]
Initiative: +9

Hooks and barbs +11 vs. AC—14 damage
  Natural 16+: The lesser hooked demon can make another *hooks and barbs* attack as a free action (and yes, this can keep going up to a maximum number of attacks equal to the escalation die +1).

AC	20	
PD	18	**HP 22 (mook)**
MD	24	

Mook: Kill one lesser hooked demon for every 22 damage you deal to the mob.

STEEL BRIGADE CHOPPER

Fires burn bright in confined spaces: this demon still thinks it's going to command its own demonic brigade some day and carve out new hellholes.

7th level mook [DEMON]
Initiative: +11

Big chopper +13 vs. AC—13 damage
  Natural even hit: 5 ongoing fire damage.
  Natural odd hit or miss: A nearby non-mook Steel Brigade demon heals 5 hit points.

AC	23	
PD	20	**HP 24 (mook)**
MD	18	

Mook: Kill one Steel Brigade chopper for every 24 damage you deal to the mob.

MINOR SERPENT DEMON

Progressing sword by sword and death by death towards a full marilith.

7th level troop [DEMON]
Initiative: +13

Four whirling swords +12 vs. AC (4 attacks)—7 damage
   Miss: 2 damage

C: Beguiling gaze +12 vs. MD (one nearby or far away unengaged enemy)—As a free action, the target immediately moves toward the minor serpent demon, attempting to engage it or get as close as possible to it
   Limited use: 1/round, as a quick action.

Terrible swords: When the escalation die is even, the minor serpent demon's crit range with melee attacks expands by a number equal to the escalation die.

AC	23	
PD	16	**HP 98**
MD	20	

BARON STEEL

It is prophesied that one day Baron Steel will fall to the Crusader, and be enslaved by him. In chains of steel, he will become the Crusader's greatest captain, until he betrays his master in the final battle of the Age—but who listens to prophecy?

Large 8th level leader [DEMON]
Initiative: +16

Massive two-handed sword +13 vs. AC (two attacks)—30 damage
   Twist the Blade: If both attacks target the same enemy, and both attacks hit, the second hit is automatically a crit.

C: Roar +12 vs. MD (1d4+1 enemies)—50 psychic damage.
   Natural 14+: Baron Steel gains a fear aura against that target (hard save ends, 16+). Foes with 48 or fewer hit points who fear Baron Steel become dazed (−4 attack) and do not benefit from the escalation die when engaged with the Baron.
   Limited Use: Once per battle

R: Fiery whip +13 vs. PD (one nearby enemy, or one far away enemy at −2 atk)—50 fire damage, and the target is dragged over to become engaged with Baron Steel.

(Group ability) For every two demons in the battle allied with Baron Steel (round up, ignore mooks), one of them can use *infernal discipline* as a free action once during the battle.

Infernal discipline (group): Choose a foe engaged with the demon. That foe may immediately make a free basic attack on the demon. If the demon is still alive, it blocks the escalation die from increasing this round.

Nastier Specials
Roar of triumph: Whenever Baron Steel scores a critical hit, he gains another use of his Roar attack.

Crack'd armor: When Baron Steel first becomes staggered, reduce his AC by 2 and give him the *fiery aura* ability.

Fiery aura: Any foes engaged with Baron Steel take 15 fire damage at the start of his turn.

AC	25	
PD	23	**HP 280**
MD	16	

THE ROCKGRUBS

The Rockgrub Clan dwell under the castle, in the tunnel-riddled crag itself. They are all born from the stone, carved into existence by a hideous demon they call Grandmother. The Rockgrubs loathe all the other demons equally, although they've supplied both the Chiding Ladies and the Revelers with treasures salvaged from the lower parts of the castle in exchange for temporary alliances against Steel's Brigade. Grandmother's long-term plan is to gnaw away at the castle's foundations one Rockgrub at a time until the whole place collapses, leaving her queen of the rubble. Currently, the Rockgrubs control the Dungeons and the Crackways.

   Strength in numbers: Most of the Rockgrubs you'll fight are mooks. If you'd like to introduce some more dangerous demons from the faction, try a frenzy demon that burrows (*13th Age* core rulebook, page 211), or take the xorn that appear on page 290 of *13th Age Bestiary 2* and reskin them as demons.

THE ROCKGRUB FACTION ABILITIES

Use these when the Red Crag Castle Random Demon Abilities table yields a faction ability.

Faction Ability 1—**Underminer:** When this demon is first staggered, part of the floor collapses beneath it. Any creatures engaged with the demon become stuck (save ends.

Faction Ability 2—**Escalating rage:** When staggered, this demon adds the escalation die to its attacks.

ROCKGRUB DEMON

Born of slime and sandstone, most Rockgrubs are blind and must hunt by smell and fumbling touch.

6th level mook [DEMON]
Initiative: +8

Blind fumble +11 vs. PD—5 damage, and the target is *Found*. The target remains *found* as long as it remains engaged with any Rockgrub demons.

Bash and smash +12 vs. AC (*found* enemies only)—20 damage

Burrow: Rockgrubs can tunnel quickly through the ground.

Nastier Specials

Marco Polo: Rockgrubs get a +4 attack bonus to *blind fumble* attacks against any characters whose players spoke out loud in this round.

AC	23	
PD	16	**HP 23**
MD	20	

Mook: Kill one Rockgrub demon mook for every 23 damage you deal to the mob.

THE CHIDING LADIES

The Chiding Ladies are a band of scholarly demons who wear masks of human flesh beneath their grey robes. They control the castle's chapel and—through a pact with the Steel Brigade—the Library Tower. When the Diabolist visits this hellhole, she resides with the Chiding Ladies, and brings them pupils for their infernal school. (Depending on your take on the Diabolist, these pupils might be:

- Spellcasters who willingly apprenticed themselves to the Diabolist, sent to study grammar, infernal theology, the heraldry and genealogy of the demon lords and other worth subjects under the harsh tutelage of the Chiding Ladies
- Children—kidnapped or offered as tribute—being raised as despoilers
- Changeling demon shapeshifters, here to learn how to disguise themselves as humans. In time, these cuckoos will replace the sons and daughters of various Imperial noble families, taking over the Empire from within
- Prisoners like captured adventurers, sent to be brainwashed and converted into the service of the Diabolist

With the Diabolist's effective backing, none of the other factions dare to attack the Chiding Ladies directly, but any attempts the Ladies make to move outside their stronghold are swiftly thwarted by impromptu alliances.

Other Chiders: If you'd like a few other versions of the Chiding Ladies to keep yourself entertained, options include a despoiler mage (*13th Age* core rulebook, page 213) and the acolyte of Thanatar from the Chaos enemies section of *13th Age Glorantha*.

THE CHIDING LADIES FACTION ABILITIES

Use these when the Red Crag Castle Random Demon Abilities table yields a faction ability.

Faction ability 1—**Consider Yourself Chided:** Once per battle, when a foe engaged with the Chiding Lady rolls a natural 1-5 on a d20, the roll becomes a natural 1 and results in a terrible fumble of some sort.

Faction ability 2—**Favorite:** Whoever slays the demon is struck by a *curse of vengeance*, and gains a 1-point negative relationship with the Diabolist. This relationship never provides benefits, only story complications, and lasts until the adventurer levels up twice or the demon has its revenge, whichever comes first.

80

1: Incoming! Pick a random adventurer to make a DC30 Dexterity check to dodge or take 2d20 regular damage and 1d20 fire damage.

2: Rain of Fire! +20 vs. PD targeting all player characters; 4d10 fire damage on a hit

3: Meteor Swarm! 1d4 incoming meteors, each one targeting a different player character. +20 vs. PD; on a hit, 1d20 regular damage and 1d20 fire damage

4: I Can Fly! The rock beneath one of the PCs wrenches free and rockets into the sky. Jump off before it launches with a DC25 Dexterity check, or stay on it and surf through the sky (counts as flying), but make a DC20 Dexterity check every round to avoid falling. Fail, and you fall a very long way and go splat (probably 4d10 damage unless you hit something soft). Oh, and if you roll a 1 on your Dexterity check, the rock explodes for 4d10 damage and *then* you fall. An especially cruel Gamemaster might say that the threshold for rock-explosion rises by 1 for every check you make (so, roll a 1 or 2 on your second check, and boom; roll 3 or less on your third, boom, and so on). And to be honest, if you're in an epic-level hellhole, you're asking for cruelty with more cruelty on top. Gamemasters, go get 'em.

5: We All Can Fly! As above, but it's 1d4+1 members of the party who end up on the same flying chunk of rock. It's a bigger, more stable surface, so the DC to stay on is a trivial DC15 (unless you're doing extravagant flying maneuvers, in which case, see above re: cruelty). The downside is when this island goes boom, it's a bigger (6d10) boom.

6: (In Some Other Universe) This is How The Dinosaurs Got TPKed: A gigantic chunk of burning rock falls out of the heavens, aimed straight towards the player characters. Rocks fall, everybody dies unless they come up with a semi-plausible way of escaping the impact zone in the next 1d4+1 rounds. (*Teleport*, flying steeds, swashbuckling, really great skill checks).

Burning Cloud Castles

The Hellgout acts like a vortex of fire, drawing in the lighter elements of the overworld and dragging them down to earth while lighting them on fire. The most common (visible) casualties of this cataclysm are the cloud castles of the giants. While these castles can tack with the wind like immense sailing ships, the drag from the hellgout is too strong for many of them to resist. Worse, when the cloud castle leaves the overworld and enters the mortal realm, it loses its magical solidity and becomes an ordinary cloud (so add "falling, burning, angry giants" to the list of hazards)—well, ordinary except for the bit where it burns like aerial pitch. Burning cloud castles are sticky and incredibly hot, and coat huge areas when they splatter on impact. (+20 vs. PD, 3d10 fire damage plus 15 ongoing fire damage).

Crazed Celestials

The cloud castles are the most visible casualties from the overworld, but they're not the only things caught and burnt up in the Hellgout. Spirits, couatls, living spells and other weird denizens of the overworld also suffer when the Hellgout catches them, and get thrown down to earth in horribly burnt or truncated forms. This mass slaughter of spirits causes all sorts of weirdness in the lands around the Hellgout (alien dreams, spontaneous magical outbursts, possession by vengeful spirits, icon dice getting swapped around, certain types of magic not working, and so on).

Earthquakes...

The ground around the Hellgout's tormented and broken. Massive earth tremors, castle-swallowing cracks, landslides, quakes... all sorts of fun, but they're the least of the dangers here.

...and Skyquakes

Skyquakes are titanic semi-magical rips in the fabric of the air. On a mundane level, they manifest as bursts of force in the sky that deal 4d20 damage to any flying creatures or objects. On a magical level, they also disrupt any *fly* spells or effects. When a skyquake hits, nothing stays flying.

Skyquakes are most common around the edges of the hellhole, preventing anyone from just flying into the middle of the hellhole. The only way to reach the heart of the hellhole is to approach from below (walk across the tormented ground, and then start climbing) or above (enter via the overworld).

...and Spellquakes

Wizard magic in the hellhole is extremely unstable. The good news is that the whole Hellgout region counts as the overworld for the purposes of abilities like the wizard's overworld Advantage class feature. The downside is that if you roll a 1 when trying to recharge a daily spell, that spell... breaks. If you're *lucky*, that's just an explosion of magical energy (3d10 force damage to everyone nearby). If you're unlucky, then the spell might stop working for *everyone* in the Empire, at least as long as the Hellgout exists, or the spell might get burnt onto your consciousness so you can't get rid of it even if you want to prepare something else, or the exploding spell breaks off a piece of your soul, and you've now got a doppelganger running around imbued with a super-charged version of the errant spell.

Against the Demons

As a known epic-tier threat , the Hellgout has attracted attention from many of the icons and from other power groups who oppose demons, or at least oppose demons destroying their section of the world. Use the following groups as potential allies and story-drivers as the PCs mount their own operations against the hellhole.

THE CRUSADER'S ARMY

The Hellgout is larger and more dangerous than any of the other hellholes yet conquered by the Crusader's forces—but the Crusader has never lacked in ambition or audacity. A garrison of the Crusader's troops watches over the edges of the hellhole, under the command of **Cremain Moor**, a veteran of the war against the demons. Cremain's served the Crusader for many years; he's old and so very tired, but the infernal hordes won't relent and so he cannot yet rest. Secretly, he still worships the gods of light as well as dark, but if his old friend and master knows of Cremain's secret faith, the Crusader has yet to act on this knowledge. Cremain's main army maintains a siege on the hellhole; a smaller force has captured a ruined town referred to as 'First Step' (see page 89) within the hellhole itself.

The Hellgout is so dangerous that few mortal troops can survive in there for long, even with protective magic. Cremain has therefore brought up reinforcements from First Triumph— bound demons, enslaved by the Crusader's magic. Pitting demon against demon is the only way to keep control of First Step, but the local forces (see below) now mistrust Cremain and the Crusader.

Even with demonic allies, the Crusader's army has no chance of capturing the hellhole through conventional assault. Cremain's orders are to contain the enemy while the Crusader or his followers capture another flying realm (possibly Battle Barge, see *13th Age* p. 267) to use as an assault platform.

THE GOLDEN ORDER

The Crusader has thousands of soldiers and hundreds of siege engines, war golems, bound demons and other monsters besieging the Hellgout. The Great Gold Wyrm's forces here are more modest. Three of his servants watch over this hellhole. Chief of them is **Emeste the Scholar**, an archaeologist and historian. She was blinded by agents of the Three, so now she's guided and aided by two halflings, **Merk** and **Mirk** (multi-classed monk/paladin and monk/demonologist respectively).

Emeste's area of expertise is the Abyss and the history of the Great Gold Wyrm. The Hellgout terrifies her beyond all else, because of the alarming resemblance it bears to certain fragmentary descriptions of the events that led to the opening of the great rift of the Abyss, the demonic invasion of the surface world, and the ensuing sacrifice of the Wyrm. Few records of that time survive—the Red Dragon's incineration of the demon army in what later became the Red Wastes ensured that. Emeste isn't certain that the Hellgout is a precursor to a much, much, much bigger hellhole or world-ending cataclysm, but she worries that the Crusader's plans to crash a flying realm into the hellhole will make things much worse.

The Host of the Overworld

The cryptic and aloof entities of the celestial realm rarely deign to interact with those from below. Cloud giants don't just look down their nose at you, they look down their entire lanky bodies, and every inch of them manages to sneer. Rainsong nagas only talk to wizards. Sphinxes communicate only in riddles or through oblique references to constellations. Silver dragons are bit more approachable, but their constant well-meaning advice and holier-than-thou attitude is wearing.

It was unheard of in this Age (outside Santa Cora, of course, where things are different) for the celestial denizens to gather in an army and make war, but that is what the Hellgout has achieved. Demons cannot easily leave a hellhole and march into the Dragon Empire, but the overworld is a different matter—demons can thrive there. (Heaven's just a Hell that's not on fire yet.) To prevent a full-scale invasion of the overworld, a loose alliance of powerful celestial entities has been gathered by **General Hatshephut**, a sphinx.

Hatshephut is a compromise candidate—the storm giants are the most militant of the local forces in the overworld, but everyone else considers the giants to be brash and dangerous and would not follow a storm giant leader. Emissaries from the Archmage advise Hatshephut—relations between the Empire and the overworld are usually mediated through the Sky Embassy in Horizon, under the Archmage's aegis.

The Local Defenders

Depending on where you've put Hellgout in your campaign, there's going to be another army nearby. Our default assumption is that it's an Imperial army, but it might be an unofficial militia, elves from the Queen's Wood, dwarves, or even orcs or animated trees or something weirder. In any case, the local interest need the Crusader's forces to keep the demons in check, but aren't happy about the Crusader bringing yet more demons to these lands.

Wait: The Diabolist?

Unless it's entirely out of character for the Diabolist of your campaign, we think that she has visited each of the factions that are fighting against the Hellgout, covertly teaching methods of warding off demonic possession, and surprisingly effective rituals that help contain the hellhole.

She has walked in disguise in the Crusader's camp. She haunts the dreams of Cremain Moor. Her agents have been seen in Horizon visiting the Sky Embassy. Just where did Mirk the Halfling get those supposedly-lost texts about the opening of the Abyss? How did these orcs and animated trees acquire the wards to stand against hellfire?

She plays long games, and a hellhole that threatens the overworld may not be in her plans.

Angels & Demons

Your campaign may or may not populate the overworld with angels. Gareth's campaign clearly does, and we've left the references to a war between angels and demons intact. If you are more in tune with the Host of the Overworld, reinterpret some of what follows as a war of storm giants & sphinxes & couatl & overworld wizards vs. demons.

The Demonic Factions

On the other side, you've got three factions of demons, each defined by its mighty leader. They've each had visits from the Diabolist as well.

Agzarrak, Breaker of Worlds is a destiny-master, a balor general who knows no peer. That's him on the cover of this *Book of Demons*, wielding his star sword. He leads the World Breakers.

The Queen of Smoke is a shadowy monarch as subtle as Agazarrak is strong. She leads the Smoke.

Gulmagul All-Eat-All will devour the cosmos, if the Hellgout gives him the chance. No one bothers with a name for his faction. It's all about his bloatiness.

The groups led by these fiends would usually fight amongst themselves, but with so many juicy external foes to fight, and even the PCs, they don't need to kill each other for sport.

Faction mechanics: As we did with the demonic factions in Red Crag Castle, we're presenting a general random demon powers table for the Hellgout with several entries that correspond to faction abilities explained in the full write-ups below.

Random Hellgout Demon Abilities (d6 for lesser demons, d8 for bigger ones)

1: *Resist fire 18+*
2: *Entropic warp*—When an enemy deals miss damage to the demon, that enemy also takes half that amount of damage.
3: Faction ability 1
4: *Fear aura*
5: Faction ability 2
6: *Teleport 1d3 times per battle*
7: *Demonic speed*
8: Faction ability 3

World Breakers

Azgarrak is the biggest and nastiest demon in the hellhole. He's a balor of prodigious size and strength, made even more powerful by a sword he forged from a star (not a fallen star, mind you—he tore that one out of the sky as a prize when the Hellgout first broke through into the overworld). His old title was Azgarrak, Despoiler of Cities, and his new sobriquet reflects how ambitious he's become. His forces are mostly concentrated on the upper levels of the hellhole.

Azgarrak's sword lets him shape destiny when he strikes, making him an impossibly successful general. Victory is inevitably yours if you've literally cut defeat as an option.

Death incarnate: Can your PCs stand up to Azgarrak? Maybe the campaign is all about stacking up blessings and advantages that allow a fight with Azgarrak to be something other than a TPK.

The angel-eating demons in Azgarrak's employ are nasty 10th level creatures. Other servants include mariliths, balors, and most any epic tier demon that knows well enough to work for the toughest leader.

WORLD BREAKER FACTION ABILITIES

These abilities are mainly for Azgarrak's followers. But Azgarrak? He probably has one or two of them.

Faction ability 1—**Resist Force 14+**

Faction ability 2—**Gate** in 1d3 allied demons, 1 or 2 levels lower.

Faction ability 3—**Call in a firestrike:** The demon may spend a standard action praying for the gunners at the Fortress of the Balor to retarget their massive gun. Roll a 20; on an 11+, the request is granted. 1d3 rounds later, anyone near the demon is hit for 300 fire damage. This power cannot be used in the Fortress of the Balor.

AZGARRAK BREAKER OF WORLDS

This is how the world ends—the overworld, first, and then the lands below, when Azgarrak crashes the sky down upon the earth.

Large 14th level wrecker [DEMON]
Initiative: +21

Starry blade +19 vs. AC—180 damage
Natural even hit: Azgarrak deals +1d20 lightning damage to the target and to one other nearby enemy of the balor's choice. For every point on the escalation die, Azgarrak may then either strike another nearby enemy with 1d20 lightning damage, or else send a creature struck by lightning flying. Creatures sent flying pop free and are knocked back.
Miss: 90 damage

C: Destiny-cutting whirlwind +19 vs. PD (up to three nearby enemies)—160 damage, and the target may no longer add the escalation die to their attacks. Victims of this attack may regain the use of the escalation die by doing something suitably heroic and dramatic, or by spending a standard action to recombobulate themselves.

R: Starry spear +19 vs. AC (one nearby or far away enemy)—150 damage, and the target is stuck (hard save ends). The target may take another 75 damage to end the stuck effect.
Miss: 100 damage

Fear aura: Foes with 192 hit points or fewer lose access to the escalation die and are dazed (−4 to attacks) when engaged with Azgarrak.

Glorious escalator: If more than half the player characters lose the use of the escalation die (because of *fear* or *destiny-cutting whirlwind*), then Azgarrak adds the escalation die to his attack rolls.

Fiery aura: At the start of Azgarrak's turn, each enemy engaged with it takes 4d12 fire damage; any die result of 10+ is kept and the die rerolled.

Flight: Azgarrak can fly.

Shadow, flame, and destiny: Azgarrak gains a +5 bonus to all defenses against attacks by far away enemies. He also gains a +5 bonus to saves.

Nastier Specials
Destiny-breaking blade: If Azgarrak scores a crit with his *starry blade* or *destiny-cutting whirlwind*, then the target takes *triple* damage. The target may drop this down to regular double damage if the target gives up the uniqueness of their One Unique Thing.

AC	**30**	
PD	**28**	**HP 1160**
MD	**26**	

Angel-Eating Demon

Azgarrak's followers are fanatical, crazed by the taste of angel meat and furiously eager to bring ruin to the overworld.

10th level troop [DEMON]
Initiative: +16

Flesh-shredding claws +15 vs. AC (two attacks) —25 damage
Special: If both *flesh-shredding claws* hit the same target, the demon may also make a *soul-devouring bite* attack on that target as a free action.

Soul-devouring bite +15 vs. MD —30 psychic damage
Natural 18+: The target is dazed (save ends).

R: Spit hellfire +15 vs MD (one nearby or far away enemy)—60 fire damage, and 15 ongoing fire damage
Limited Use: 1/battle

Frenzy: If an angel-eating demon's natural attack roll is equal to or less than the escalation, the demon enters a frenzy. When frenzied, the demon gains an extra standard action each round, but all its defenses drop by 2.

Soul eater: Whenever the demon dazes a foe, it gains another use of *spit hellfire.*

AC	26	
PD	24	**HP 216**
MD	20	

The Smoke

Azgarrak's great rival—and great ally—is the **Queen of Smoke**. She might be a marilith, or an exceptionally talented despoiler, or even the Diabolist herself. She wears masks and magical disguises, and is everywhere and nowhere on the lower levels. Her current objective is to drive the Crusader's forces out of First Step. After that, well, the Crusader's spies have spotted smoke-shrouded demons performing arcane rituals around the base of the pillar of fire. It's clear that the Queen has some longer-term plan, one that likely involves betraying Azgarrak once he has broken open the overworld.

Strange allies: Given the Queen's mysterious nature, why not recruit devils as well as demons? See page 172 of *13 True Ways* for the original write-up of the smoke devil, especially for its *free-form cover ability—Insinuate.* We've provided an upgraded version of the smoke devil below that has either been suborned into or volunteered for the Queen's retinue. Note: No random demon abilities for these devils unless you're truly enamored of the Queen.

The Smoke Faction Abilities

These abilities are mainly for the demons who follow the Queen of Smoke.

But free to give the Queen of Smoke any or all of these abilities, as nasty specials, just because.

*Faction ability 1—***Pain in flame**: Any creature engaged with this demon at the start of its turn takes 2d10 fire damage. Retain and reroll 10s.
*Faction ability 2—***Refuge in fire**: *Resist fire 18+*, and the first time the demon resists damage from a fire attack, it gains a +1 bonus to all its defenses until the end of the battle.
*Faction ability 3—***Strength in smoke**: Once per battle as a standard action, *gate* in 1d3 strangler demons.

Queen of Smoke

There's no smoke without ire.

Double-strength 12th level spoiler [DEMON]
Initiative: +20
Vulnerability: force

Smoke claws +17 vs. PD (2 attacks)—75 damage
Natural 18+: The target begins to melt into smoke. Start making last gasp saves. If the target dies, it becomes a smoke shade (see below).
Miss: 30 damage

C: Smoke bolts +17 vs. PD (1d4+1 nearby or far away creatures)—50 fire damage
Hit or miss: Summon/create a smoke shade engaged with the target. It takes its turn immediately after the Queen.
Natural 16+: Summon/create another smoke shade engaged with the target.
Limited use: Usable only when the escalation die is 0 or even.

C: Choke +17 vs. PD (1 nearby creature)—20 damage, and the target becomes *hampered* (save ends)
Natural 16+: The save to end the *hampered* effect becomes hard (16+).
Special: The Queen of Smoke may use this attack as a quick action

Hard to hit: Any attack that hits the Queen of Smoke has a 50% chance of striking a nearby smoke shade instead.

Lost in the smoke: As a move action, the Queen of Smoke may teleport to swap places with any of her smoke shades.

Flight: The Queen of Smoke flies with terrible speed and perfect agility.

Resist damage 16+: She has *resist damage 16+* to all attacks except force damage.

Nastier Specials

Smoke in your face: If the Queen of Smoke moves or teleports into engagement with a foe, she may make a free *choke* attack on that enemy.

AC	28	
PD	22	**HP 500**
MD	26	

SMOKE SHADE

Are they her spies, or her eyes? Her guards, or her fists?

10th level troop [DEMON]
Initiative: +20

Smoky claws +15 vs. AC—50 damage

Sneaky: If a melee attack on a smoke shade misses, the shade may pop free.

Resist damage 16+: Smoke shades have *resist damage 16+* to all attacks except force damage.

Summoned: Smoke shades have no independent existence—they are created by the Queen of Smoke. If she is defeated, all smoke shades disperse. (As more-or-less summoned creatures, they might be vulnerable to banishing rituals, counter-magic and similar weirdness, but good luck making time for a ritual.)

AC	25	
PD	20	**HP 54**
MD	20	

STRANGLER DEMON

In bright light, you can see that they look like wispy clouds of smoke with very solid, very strong hands. In twilight, all you see is darkness as those hands close around your neck.

11th level blocker [DEMON]
Initiative: +20

Grab +16 vs. PD—50 damage, and the demon grabs onto its target. The grabbed foe cannot move except to teleport, pop free, or attempt to disengage, and disengage attempts take a −5 penalty unless the creature hit the demon with an attack this turn.

Resist damage 16+: when *not* abducting a victim, strangler demons have *resist damage 16+* to all attacks except force damage.

Abduction: If a demon has a grabbed target at the *start* of its turn, both target and demon vanish from the battlefield and appear in a demonic pocket extradimensional space. In this place, the demon's true form—that of an armored warrior wielding a sword—becomes visible. The demon loses its *resist damage* power in this pocket dimension, but gains the *sword of sorrow* and *time mastery* attacks. Victim and demon are both ejected from the pocket dimension when:

- The victim dies
- The demon becomes staggered or dies
- The demon voluntarily releases its victim
- The victim uses a standard action and succeeds at a DC30 check to escape (Strength to punch through the walls of

reality; Intelligence to improvise a magical ritual; Wisdom to trick the demon; Charisma to escape through sheer force of will).

Neither demon or victim can be targeted by outsiders while in the pocket dimension.

Sword of sorrow +16 vs. MD—60 psychic damage, and the victim sees visions of friends and allies in the real world dying (either through the attacks of demons, or through sheer old age).
  Natural attack roll exceeds target's Wisdom: The target is also dazed (save ends)

C: Time mastery +16 vs. PD—80 damage, and the target ages by 1d10 years. Short-lived creatures (humans, half-orcs, tieflings) lose 3 recoveries; long-lived races (dwarves, gnomes, halflings, half-elves) lose 2 recoveries; immortal or thereabouts (elves, forgeborn) lose 1 recovery. On the bright side, the victim may roll to recharge magic items and spells.

AC	27	
PD	25	**HP 250**
MD	21	

Queen-touched Smoke Devil

Most smoke devils specialize in getting where they're not supposed to be and murdering people who are supposed to be safe. No one is safe in the Hellgout, and don't these devilish allies of the Queen know it.

11th level troop [DEVIL]
Initiative: +14

Dire embrace +16 vs. PD—60 poison damage
  Full embrace: If the target is the only creature engaged with the smoke devil, the attack deals 120 poison damage instead.
  Miss: 25 poison damage.

Ember of hate: Each time the smoke devil hits an enemy, the embers floating in the center of its body glow more brightly. Once per battle as a free action during its turn, the devil can make an *ember burst* attack. It also makes this attack as an interrupt action when it drops to 0 hp.
  Ember burst +16 vs. PD (each enemy engaged with the devil)—The target takes 20 fire damage for each creature hit by the smoke devil earlier in the battle (max 60 damage; remember to track this).

Devil's due (Formless): When you choose to add the escalation die to an attack against a smoke devil, it gains *resist damage 16+* against the attack.

Flight: Smoke devils drift and eddy as if blown by an evil wind.

Resist fire 13+: When a fire attack targets this creature, the attacker must roll a natural 13+ on the attack roll or it only deals half damage.

Nastier Specials
Smokey retreat: A smoke devil can "take 12" on disengage checks, taking a natural result of 12 instead of rolling (which normally would allow it to disengage automatically from up to two enemies).

AC	25	
PD	25	**HP 360**
MD	25	

Gulmagul All-Eat-All

The third 'faction' is led by the corpulent and floaty **Gulmagul All-Eat-All**, who grows whenever he eats. He's usually found orbiting the pillar of fire as one of the flying rock islands, but he sometimes descends to pick up reinforcements from the Abyss and then carries them up to Azgarrak's fortress in the sky. When the hellhole's under attack, he lumbers over to drop off more demons there too, although so far First Step's catapults and demon-bane ballista bolts have kept him away from there.

Gulmagul's ultimate desire is to eat a Koru behemoth and become the largest predator in existence. He will break the world by eating it.

I'm with the big guy: Gulmagul cares a lot less about having followers than the other two Hellgout commanders, but he still has plenty of them, all of whom applaud his all-consuming ways and hope to learn the trick themselves. Any nasty demon will do. Non-demons don't last long around him. (Burp.)

Some of Gulmagul's followers kick around on the various flying islands of Hellgout. More are found on his back!

Gulmagul All-Eat-All Faction Abilities

These abilities are not for Gulmagul itself!
*Faction ability 1—***Bloopblip:** When the demon is first staggered, it splits in two. These new demons each have ¼ the starting hit points of the original demon.
*Faction ability 2—***Gimme!:** Staggered foes are vulnerable to the demon.
*Faction ability 3—***Feeding time:** Once per battle when the escalation die is 2+, the demon may teleport itself and any engaged creatures to the back of Gulmagul.

GULMAGUL

ALL-EAT-ALL! ALL-EAT-ALL! ALL-EAT-ALL!

Considerably bigger than huge 12th level landmass [DEMON]
Initiative: +11

Massive jaws +17 vs. AC—300 damage
Miss: 100 damage

C: Gulmagul's roar +16 vs. MD (all nearby enemies)—75 damage
Natural 14+: The target is dazed until the end of their next turn

R: Eyebeams +16 vs. PD (one or two nearby or far away enemies)—200 fire damage, and 20 ongoing fire damage (save ends)

Insanely big: Gulmagul is up there with the tarrasque in terms of sheer size. Characters can hop onto his back and move across him—he's a landmass as well as a monster. Gulmagul is immune to opportunity attacks. Disengaging from Gulmagul is easy (6+). Gulmagul cannot use his *massive jaws* or *eyebeams* attacks against creatures clinging to him, but he can use the two following attacks as free actions, one per round.

Tentacles +16 vs. PD (1d3 attacks, each one targeting a different creature on Gulmagul's back)—50 damage, and the target pops free and is sent flying through the air (opening the target to an *eyebeams* or *massive jaws* attack now or next round.)

Secondary mouths +16 vs. AC (two or more attacks, each one targeting a different creature on Gulmagul's back)—75 damage

Flying realm: Gulmagul can fly, or at least drift steadily.

Teeth beneath: If a single attack inflicts 100 or more damage on Gulmagul, he permanently gains an extra mouth, increasing his number of *secondary mouth* attacks by 1.

Nastier Specials
I'm not sure those are mouths: When Gulmagul is first staggered, summon 2d6 hooked demon mooks, +1 per *secondary mouth.*

AC	28	
PD	26	**HP 1111**
MD	22	

LOCATIONS

Getting from one flying island to the next is tricky. If you can fly, you can try dodging skyquakes (p. 81) and flying demons. Otherwise, the thing to do is wait until the next island's orbit brings it close to your current perch, and jump. Ride the thermals from hell, and hope that they give you enough lift to reach across the gap.

THE PILLAR OF FIRE

It's a roaring, writhing, furious eruption of hellfire. It's not perfectly vertical—it whips this and that like the world's biggest candle-flame, scorching the orbiting flying realms when it gets too close. Fire-resistant demons and elemental horrors climb up the inside of the pillar, straining to reach the overworld.

Anything thrown into the pillar is destroyed unless it's got astounding magical protection—these infernal fires could burn a red dragon to ash.

THE BASE OF THE PILLAR

The circle of broken stones and ash around the pillar is home to demons under the banner of the Queen of Smoke. Their queen is everywhere here; the smoke from the burning lands is so thick and acrid that it's impossible to see more than a few feet. The smoke is opportunistic—if a traveler takes a wrong turn, the smoke thickens and twists to compound the error and lure the unlucky soul into a crevasse or fiery pit. If an adventurer takes a breath at the wrong time, the smoke invades the lungs and congeals there as black tar. (Mechanically, any rolls of a 1-3 here get exploited by the smoke in some way. A botched attack might be redirected against an ally; a dismally failed save might leave the PC dazed by a coughing fit).

The caves and cairns here conceal hundreds of demons, some of whom have the gift of *truesight* and can see through the smoke. These seers lead and direct hunting packs of their fellows to find any intruders who try crossing the Base of the Pillar.

FIRST STEP

First Step is the largest of the hellhole's flying realms—it's a huge slab of bedrock that floats at an awkward angle around the pillar. One edge of First Step often tilts low enough to scrape through the rubble at the base of the pillar, cutting fresh scars into the ruin on the ground. The topmost side of the slab still has some scorched farmland clinging to it, along with the ruins of a small town.

The town was formerly called Highmarket, but now it's also called First Step. The Crusader's forces have conquered the town and are dug in there, enduring attacks from the Queen of Smoke's forces below and from demons vomited out by Gulmagul above. Bound vrocks and elemental sorcerers guard the walls of First Step, brewing up winds to keep the town clear of smoke.

THE BROKEN MEN

The next highest flying realms are called the Broken Men. This was once a single flying realm that broke in two, so now it resembles two men wrestling in the air, surrounded by a halo of smaller debris. The demons of this realm are fiercely hostile towards everyone, even the demons of the other Broken Man, and hurl barbed spears, poisonous darts and explosive eyeballs at anyone who comes close. Their enmity animates the stones of the Broken Men—the two flying islands snap and smash together with murderous intent, deliberately crushing flying creatures and ships between the rocks.

THE SKY GARDEN

From a distance, the Sky Garden looks like a blessed oasis of calm and growth compared to the fire-blasted madness of the rest of the hellhole. It's a verdant flying realm of green trees and little lakes, girdled in starlight. The Sky Garden was a flying realm of the overworld, dragged down into the hellhole when the attack on the skies began. The island was home to various celestial spirits and creatures who liked to rest here; some of these entities are still trapped here, unable to escape the hellhole.

Nalfeshnees and other demon horrors have taken up residence in the Garden, and delight in wounding the trees and defiling the little streams and lakes. Adventurers who slay these demons may be rewarded with blessings from the hidden spirits.

SKY GARDEN BLESSINGS

1: The ability to *fly* until the next full heal-up.

2: Auspicious horoscope—roll 2d20 and take the best result when making a d20 roll. Usable three times.

3: Overworld blessing—all your daily abilities become recharge 16+ until your next full heal-up.

4: Divine secrets. Gain one daily or recharge spell of your level or lower from the cleric class. You can cast this spell until your next full heal-up.

5: *Truesight* until your next full heal-up.

6: Celestial vigor. Until your next heal-up, whenever you use a recovery, you shine with positive energy. All nearby allies gain temporary hit points equal to your level.

7: You can now permanently talk to birds.

8: Celestial paramour. One of the spirits falls in love with you, and—greatly daring—follows you out of the Sky Garden.

GULMAGUL ALL-EAT-ALL

This isn't a flying realm—it's a gigantic demon the size of a flying realm. Gulmagul All-Eat-All's hide swarms with lesser demons, and he is usually content to let his parasites deal with intruders. He only wakes up and fights whenever a particular dangerous, or particularly tasty foe shows up. He keeps careful watch on the Edge of the Abyss.

Gulmagul had a write-up as a monster, as opposed to geography, a couple pages above.

THE EDGE OF THE ABYSS

The sixth flying island in the chain is almost completely lost in the pillar of fire. Three-quarters of the realm is inside the flames, leaving only a small ledge of stone on the edge of the abyss. Adventurers hoping to move upwards need to cling to the ledge and pray that the flying realm does not do any deeper into the fires while they wait for Wrackspell's orbit to bring it within reach.

Given the intensity of the flames, no-one knows if there are two portals to the Abyss in there, or if there's just one that runs all the way through the realm. Either way, if the Crusader intends to conquer this hellhole, then he'll need to march his armies into the fires that constantly blast and burn this floating island.

Occasionally, the flying realm tumbles or is buffeted by the pillar of flame, and that triggers immense jets of fire, ash and molten rock that shoot out for miles beyond the limits of the hellhole, like an eruption from a flying volcano.

WRACKSPELL

Arcane magic draws from the overworld. Some wizards command magical forces with shouted spells and emphatic gestures with their mighty staffs. Others coax it down with whispered incantations and subtle flick-of-the-wrist wand movements.

Demons rarely get to study the overworld up close. Think of the Wrackspell as a despoiler mage research laboratory dedicated to answering the question *"what happens if instead commanding or coaxing magical forces, you torture them until they do what you say? Can barbed wire be as effective as wand or staff?"* So far, signs point to yes. The despoiler mages of Wrackspell work feverishly to take advantage of their unique opportunity, and any captured wizards or scholars are put to work here. There are demonic slave-drivers who are attuned to the subtleties of abstruse calculations, and know to hold back the whip when the wizard-slave is mentally calculating some arcane formula, and to inflict pain the instant the slave's thoughts slip to futile dreams of escape.

Fortress of the Balor

Azgarrak built his stronghold from broken stars and hell-forged bronze plates. Demonic artificers from Wrackspell have created a cunning mechanism, a cannon made from mirrors and rune-scored binding rings, that can channel and redirect the hellfire of the pillar of flame into a weapon. The workings of this siege cannon take up a third of the palace; the rest is split between dungeons and torture chambers for captured celestials, and barracks and armories for Azgarrak's troops.

Star's End

The last of the hellhole's flying realms was shattered by a test firing of Azgarrak's death ray. Now, it's a burning ring of smaller flying rocks, where the scorched undead remains of celestials battle with both their surviving former compatriots, and the demonic hordes from the Fortress of the Balor who press on towards the edge of the overworld.

CHAPTER 4

CITADELS OF THE ICONS

Two icons make their homes in hellholes. A third, the Great Gold Wyrm, probably doesn't count because you wouldn't refer to his hellish battlefield as a *home*.

The Diabolist has resided in the fetid, treacherous swamps of Hellmarsh since before the beginning of the current Age, although in all that time only a few brave souls have returned from visiting her eerie citadel. The Crusader came to prominence only a few years ago when his forces conquered First Triumph, but his terrifying fortress has drawn thousands of mercenaries and warriors to his banner.

As First Triumph is much, much more accessible than the Citadel of the Diabolist, let's start there.

FIRST TRIUMPH

First Triumph is both fortress and city. To call it a 'castle' or 'citadel' is to ignore the thousands of merchants and craftsmen who live within it. There are markets and crafthalls, temples and libraries, even mines and farms within the walls of First Triumph. At the same time, calling it a walled city is a misnomer—every building is built to be as strong as the strongest keep, and whole districts of the city are indoors. Space is at an incredible premium here; everything is cramped, or built on top or or under something else. Not an inch of the castle is wasted space. It is possible to spend years in First Triumph and never see the pallid sun outside. The city is as self-sufficient as the Crusader could make it. Magical gardens and vats grow food in the dungeons below, and deep shafts reach down into the freshwater seas of the Underworld.

The inevitable conclusion is that First Triumph was designed to endure a siege of demons. If the Great Gold Wyrm fails and the hordes come rushing out of the Abyss, they might conquer Axis and Horizon, Santa Cora and even the Necropolis, but not First Triumph. This fortress will outlast the rest of the Empire.

Lawful, and evil: Life within First Triumph is strictly regimented. The whole city is under martial law, enforced by the Crusader's warriors. They are empowered to deliver summary judgment on the spot to lawbreakers and troublemakers. Criminals are customarily handed over to the temples of the Dark Gods as slaves or sacrifices. If you behave in perfect accordance with the Crusader's will, then First Triumph is the safest and most equitable city in all the world. Only deviates have anything to fear from the inquisitors.

Enslaved demons: Demons are everywhere in First Triumph. The Iron Spike (page 98) keeps them bound to the Crusader, reducing them from vicious warriors of chaos to wretched slaves of law. The divine energies of the Crusader and the corrosive power of the spike means that the demons only last a few years before they waste away to nothingness, so the Crusader gets as much work out of them as he can before they perish. Demons don't need to eat or sleep to survive, so food and rest is denied them. Every unpleasant or rote job in the city is done by demon slaves; the massive gates are pushed closed by demons, and the forges and fires kept burning by demons. Monsters that once struck terror into the souls of anyone who encountered them are here made into beasts of burden.

As so much of the drudge work is done by demons, it frees the mortal population of the city to attend to other matters, and that usually means training. Officially, there are no civilians in First Triumph, and everyone is expected to master some useful combat style or talent to contribute to the war effort. (Like any city, of course, First Triumph has its share of thieves, wastrels, criminals and traitors, but they have to be circumspect in their activities to avoid being arrested and punished). Military drills and discipline are a constant in First Triumph.

The other hellholes under the Crusader's control are not as populous or as fortified as First Triumph, but if you listen to the Crusader's propaganda, it is only a matter of time before they too are converted into similar sanctuaries, bastions for some future apocalyptic war. Depending on your campaign, it might be more interesting to play that First Triumph is somehow unique and the other conquered hellholes are struggling to duplicate its success.

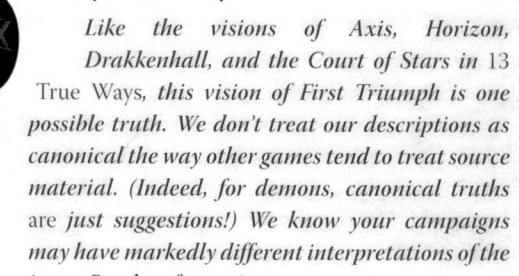

Many True Ways

Like the visions of Axis, Horizon, Drakkenhall, and the Court of Stars in 13 True Ways, *this vision of First Triumph is one possible truth. We don't treat our descriptions as canonical the way other games tend to treat source material. (Indeed, for demons, canonical truths are just suggestions!) We know your campaigns may have markedly different interpretations of the icons. Read on for variants..*

The Outer Barbican

Visitors to First Triumph must pass through this outermost ring of fortifications to enter the city proper. Although First Triumph is surrounded on all sides by miles of blasted hellscape, there is always a long line of people desperate to get in. Most come from the lands north of First Triumph, and came fleeing the Orc Lord's armies and the threat of hellholes elsewhere in the Empire. They fear that the end of the Age approaches, and that only the Crusader has the strength and will to defend them and keep them safe.

From other gates issue the armies of the Crusader, marching off to conquer other hellholes or garrison the lands around First Triumph, for the people of that region increasingly look to the Crusader and not the Emperor as their ruler.

Even those loyal to the Crusader must submit to a lengthy battery of tests to pass through the Barbican. Those who are not part of the crusade face even more rigorous scrutiny—interrogations, customs inspections, magical examination, even torture and bloodletting to ensure that a prospective visitor is not a demon in disguise. Spellcasters and other powerful individuals may be assigned a 'guide' while in First Triumph, often a bound demon. This guide's only purpose is to ensure that the visitor does not interfere with the war effort, and is of no use in navigating the city's labyrinthine corridors and alleyways.

Bribery to hasten passage through the Barbican is forbidden; volunteering for temporary service in the war effort is acceptable. The master of the guards here is a dwarf woman named **Stamper**; she is served by a swarm of magical moths that spy on visitors and report to her in rustling whispers of their wings.

On average, it takes a full day to get through the security checks of the Barbican. If you're unlucky. . . well, there are prisons here crammed with those who are suspect in the eyes of the Crusader. If they are not demons, then surely they will not mind being held for months or years until the truth of their souls can be ascertained.

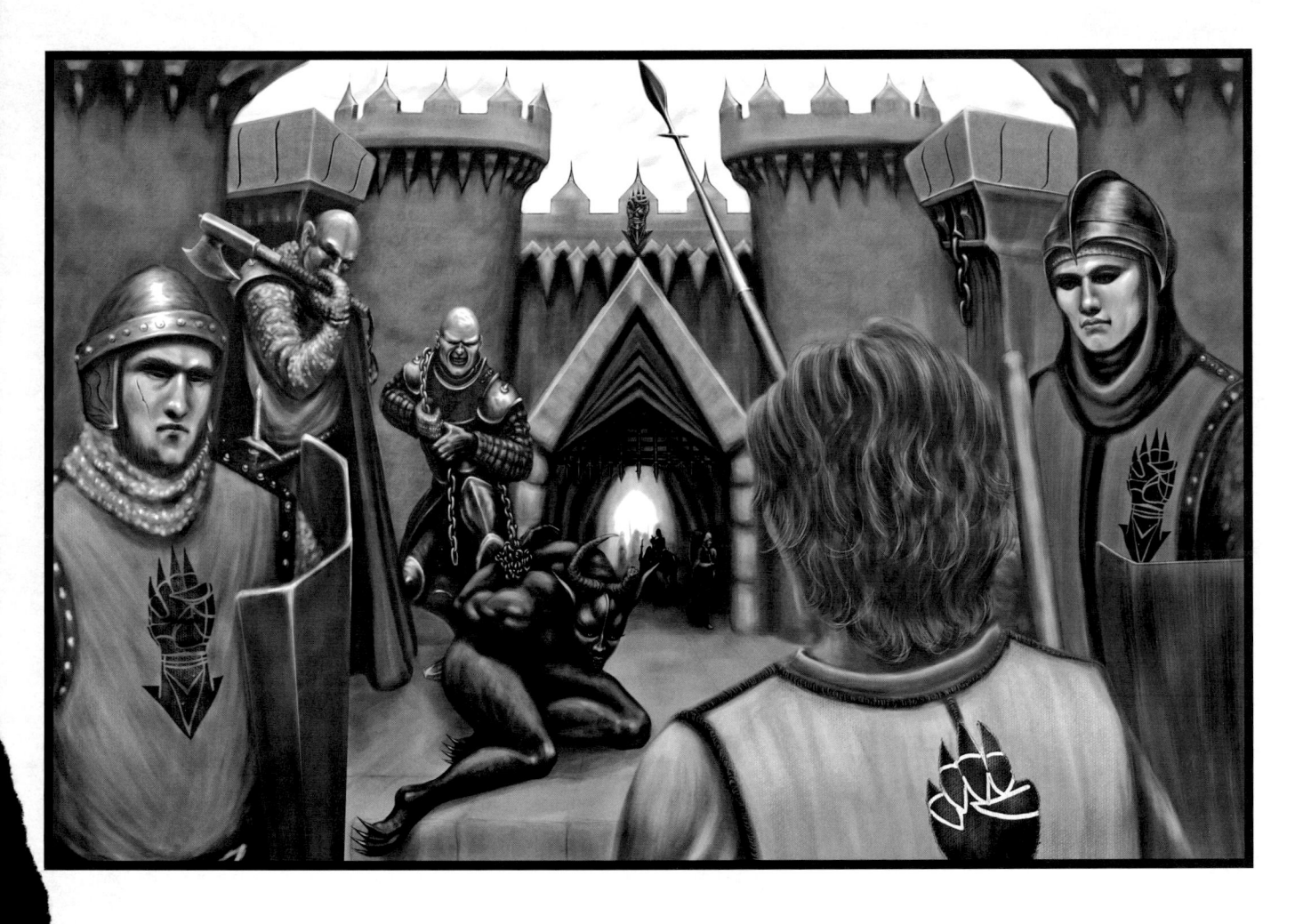

Muster

The Muster district is the most cosmopolitan part of First Triumph—if you're not part of the Crusader's followers, then this is usually as far as you go. It most resembles a crowded slum in Axis or Drakkenhall, only with more enslaved demons and more clerics openly proselytizing for the dark gods. The town's main market is in Muster; like the Floating Market, all sorts of strange demonic tinctures and spell components can be bought here, but certain items are strictly controlled by the Crusader's guards.

Many of those who come to Muster have nowhere else to go. There are alms-houses here where the starving and desperate can get a bath, a square meal and a place to sleep, as long as they swear to join the crusade when their strength returns.

Muster Inns

Staying in an inn in Muster is a huge faux pas. It's a public declaration that you're not part of the Crusader's army, that you're a stinking parasite here to profit from the war effort, or an effete coward who refuses to fight to save the world, or a follower of those loathsome and deceptive gods of light. Or maybe you're a *secret demon worshipper*, and it'd be best for the world if you got knifed in some alleyway. No witnesses, somehow, even though First Triumph is grotesquely overcrowded.

Wise visitors to First Triumph know to stay with friends, or find a private room outside an inn. The inns here cater mostly to merchants. Three of note:

- **The Last Call** is supposedly for those who have come to join the Crusader's army, but want one last night of freedom and debauchery before submitting to martial discipline. The inn has arrangements with certain temples in the Dark Temple, so guests can participate in rites of unknown pleasures, or in sacraments involving strange fumes and drugs. Of late, most of the inn's clientele are debased wealthy pleasure-seekers from Glitterhaegen who've grown jaded by the entertainments offered even in Shadowport.
- **The Pot and Kettle** is a more subdued establishment, catering for merchants and diplomats from Axis, Glitterhaegen or Forge. No demons are allowed on the premises, and the doors are guarded by trustworthy dwarves. It's a little island of sanity in the middle of the Muster. There's even a secret temple to the gods of light in the attic.
- **The Inn of the Insult**, also known as the Inn-Sult, is hard to pin down. It moves around the Muster, materializing in

The Armies of the Crusade

The Crusader commands an army the like of which the world has not seen in many an Age. He has no compunction about the use of any weapon or sorcery. Morality does not bind him, nor does mercy hold him back.

The majority of his army are human, or mostly human, with members of most every humanoid race as the exception. A careful inspection might reveal that leadership positions are disproportionately occupied by non-humans. That may be because exceptional (in one way or another) members of the non-human races are drawn to the Crusader's service, while desperation is the lowest common denominator among human followers.

There are mercenaries and veteran soldiers drawn to his banner by the prospect of plunder. There are refugees and vengeance-seekers who lost everything they had to demons or orcs, and now want to fight back. Then, there are those saved by dark magic. Wounded warriors given new limbs harvested from demons, broken people armed with twisted implements of magic, the sick and the dying given a new, abhorrent form of life. Experiments in magical augmentation and cross-breeding that would not be countenanced in Horizon or Santa Cora are common-place among the Crusader's troops. Anything is permissible.

Alongside these mortal warriors march the demon slaves. Bound by iron spikes and rune-engraved chains, these demons were taken from conquered hellholes. They fight until their physical shells are ground to dust, and then their demonic spirits are used as fuel for spells and burnt up rather than allowed to return to Hell. Demon troops need no food or rest, so the Crusader's armies sometimes march faster than mortal forces. Swollen demon-beasts serve as mounts, as transports, even flying machines.

Now that the Crusader has a manufacturing base in First Triumph, he has added war-golems and enchanted siege engines to his arsenal. These monstrous constructs have the double virtue of being both mindless and soulless, rendering them immune to the worst hazards and deceptions of the hellholes. In obtaining the rare magical metals needed for mass construction of golems, the Crusader may come into conflict with the Dwarf King.

The Crusader does not turn away monsters, as long as they are willing to submit to his discipline. There are a few dragons—whites and blues, mostly—in the army. There are orcs, trolls and ogres, few of whom understand the Crusader's ultimate goal, but willing to hang around as long as there's a prospect of booty and smashing. There are hosts of undead, although these are entirely made from the fallen bodies and souls of the Crusader's existing soldiers, for the Crusader fears that recruiting older, more powerful undead would leave his forces open to subversion by the Lich King.

Finally, the Crusader marches under the banner of the dark gods, and their emissaries and emanations must be counted among his troops. Invisible things lope along in the train of the army, materializing in the mortal world when enough blood is shed.

And this army of horrors is perhaps five days' march from Axis. If the Crusader were not sworn to destroy all demons, he could be a greater threat to the Empire's capital than the Orc Lord.

one doorway or another. Unless, of course, it's in Horizon today. It gets homesick, you see. It all began when the Archmage paid an unexpected visit to First Triumph. The Crusader offered the Archmage the same sort of meager bedding that any other beggar gets when they show up at the Muster. Irritated, the Archmage snapped his fingers and summoned a luxurious inn from Horizon and spent the night there. The Crusader hates this intrusion into his fortress, but has yet to find a way to get rid of the Inn. The only way to find the Inn-sult is to have the aid or favor of the Archmage's servants.

DARK TEMPLE

The Dark Temple isn't a single building (yet—there are ever-more bridges, walkways and shrines being built as the army grows, so perhaps one day a Dark Priestess will emerge, a consort to the Crusader, and she will raise a towering cathedral of black basalt mortared with demons' blood and adorned with the broken symbols of the gods of light, a sacrificial altar reaching to the heavens where a thousand offerings are made daily to the dreadful and sullen dark powers, glorious and terrible beyond measure and . . . .).

Sorry. Outbursts of religious mania often happen in this district, even in parentheses. It's not uncommon to hear some worshipper chanting uncontrollably in a forgotten and blasphemous tongue. The children of the district gather to laugh at those caught up in the rapture of the darkness, for there are many children here. Orphans, mostly, taken in by the dark priests to be trained as clerics, or by the monks to be trained as assassins. Others were born here, conceived in the orgiastic rites of certain temples. Not all the gods here are doleful and hateful—there are pleasures here forbidden by the gods of light, and blessings that cannot be obtained by Santa Cora. The Dark Temple is also the pleasure-quarter of the fortress—gambling, drinking, dancing and other diversions are forbidden in First Triumph except when operated by a dark temple.

Other parts of the district are less welcoming.

Do not stray there.

Know them by their silence.

Personalities: The two most important clerics are the urbane dark elf **Lady Sjanthis** and **Boark Godheaded**. Lady Sjanthis is also called the Soulless for she has deliberately severed her connection with the Elf Queen. She claims that her soul is now the Crusader, and she will live or die with him.

Boark's devotion to the dark powers is even more dramatic. He removed his own head as part of a cult ceremony, and now carries it around under his arm. He's not undead—he claims to be sustained by constant healing spells from the gods. Sometimes, the face of one dark god or another manifests above his bloody neck-stump.

WAILING YARDS

Demons are kept in the Wailing Yards. Part slave pen, part occult laboratory, part stockyard, and all nightmare. The worst are the containment structures where ruined demons are stored, demons who have lost all physical form and all psychic integrity, reduced to nothing more than bodiless screaming malice.

Due to the population pressure in First Triumph, new barracks and tenements have been built in close proximity to the containment buildings. Who'd notice a few more madmen in this hellish place?

TRUTH

Truth is a horribly overcrowded district of barracks, rookeries, tenements and towers. Most of the city's population live here.

In the middle of Truth is a large open square called the Mercy Pits. These pits contain all manner of prisoners. Some are demons; some are justly incarcerated prisoners. Others inmates are wholly innocent—refugees, children, animals, even members of the Crusader's army. Their screams and pleas for help can be heard throughout Truth.

Next to each pit are the various mercies, like a flask of cold water, some food, a key to open the grating or a rope ladder so the prisoner can climb out. The Pits are unguarded, so it's perfectly possible for someone to go down and free a prisoner.

No-one ever does. The Crusader's first lesson is that mercy is a weakness, that love is madness. There is nothing that those prisoners could ever do with their paltry lives that would be more valuable, in the long run, than teaching this lesson to the people of the city.

OTHER TRIUMPHS

If this take on First Triumph as a massively overcrowded recruiting station/last ditch sanctuary/occult arcology doesn't fit with your conception of the Crusader, how about these variants?

The Empty Fortress: The Crusader's giant fortress in First Triumph is mostly empty. He's got space here to house thousands of followers. He's got armories full enough of weapons and armor to outfit a dozen armies. He's got stockpiles of supplies to endure a siege for centuries. He's only got a handful of followers here, skulking amid the empty halls, but he's clearly planning for the long term.

The Silent Fortress: The fortress is only for the Crusader's forces. There are no markets here, no thronged districts full of non-combatants. This fortress is more like a monastery, inhabited only by disciplined warriors, quiet assassins, and whispering dark spellcasters. Visitors aren't welcome.

The Forbidden Fortress: As above, but the fortress is surrounded by a shanty town of refugees, beggars and traders. Sometimes, the Crusaders' forces open the gates and let a few supplicants in, but otherwise they ignore the sea of humanity that crowds against their walls, seeking shelter from the terrors of the hellhole.

HARVESTER DEEPS

The land outside First Triumph is poisonous, and nothing good can ever grow there. The fortress relies on these artificial cave-farms to feed its inhabitants. Such techniques are common in the dwarf-lands, but the Crusader doesn't have time to cultivate a mushroom cave for decades before it's ready for the harvest. Instead, he uses magic to hasten the growth of plants, and ground-up demon and bone meal as fertilizer. Animals are also farmed here—they are given to the dark temples first for sacrifices, and then their meat is collected and salted so it can supply armies in the field. Such unnatural growth requires druidic magic, and if the High Druid will not provide the blessings the Crusader needs, then he attempts to take them by force.

Below the farm caves are mines that feed the fortress' ever-growing hunger for ore.

NEVERSLEEP

The industrial counterpart to the Harvester Deeps, Neversleep is home to the castle's forges, workshops, tanneries and alchemical breweries. As the name suggests, the forges are never silent; when one smith is exhausted, another takes her place, and the demon servants never tire. Illumination is provided in both the Harvester Deeps and Neversleep by harsh magical lights held aloft by bound imps.

IMPERIAL COMPOUND

The only garden in all of First Triumph is found here, in this little walled compound. The Imperial Compound is the private residence of the Emperor's liaison with the Crusader, an old gnomish diplomat called **Demby Greenshoes**. Demby has the demeanor of a lovable, forgetful grandpa and rarely argues with anyone. He's not completely fluffy—he's cynical about all religions, light and dark, and he was an infamous spymaster in Shadowport before the Emperor sent him here.

Demby knows that a direct confrontation with the Crusader wouldn't end well for him (or for the Empire), so he liaises with a light touch, and relies on deniable adventurers to sort out problems that might cause friction between the Crusader and the rest of the Empire. Demby's bodyguard, **Cecilia**, is a shapeshifting bronze dragon.

THE SPIKES

The Iron Spike is right in the heart of the fortress. It's a single huge chunk of metal driven right into the remains of the now-sealed portal to Hell. How the Crusader got a hundred-foot tall metal spike into position is a mystery, as is the origin of the spike. It's covered in magical runes and wards. The spike seems to pulse as magical energies flow though it—it may even be alive to some degree, an artificial demon king that's taken command of all the demons in the hellhole. Removing the spike might cause the hellhole to open up again. Chains run from rings on the spike to other, smaller binding nodes and wards, keeping the more powerful demons in check.

Demons cannot approach the spike. If they get too close, it absorbs them. There are weird bumps and distorted metal stains where a demon trespassed too near the spike.

The other spikes are made of wood and stone, not metal—they're towers that rise alongside the Iron Spike, where the Crusader's sorcerers and wizards study the arcane arts.

TOWER

The main keep is called Tower. Not the tower, just Tower.

All of Tower is forbidden to outsiders, except the Crusader's audience room. It's a simple, unadorned chamber with a large round table and a few ordinary chairs. The Crusader has no throne, no servants, no crown or title. He has his cause, and that is enough.

Tower is wound around with potent defensive spells of all kinds—divine blessings from the dark gods, arcane wards made by the best wizards, demonic power siphoned from the spike, and even forbidden magics from previous Ages. From the summit of the Tower, the Crusader can see anywhere in the Dragon Empire, and can direct his armies from afar.

THE CRUSADER'S SECRET WEAPON

The spikes are part of whatever secret technique the Crusader uses to seal hellholes. The spike not only 'caps' the portal to hell, closing the hellhole, it also works as a giant binding spell, seizing control of the remaining demons that came through that portal. These demons are utterly bound to the spike, and are incapable of breaking free or refusing the commands of the Crusader's servants.

This binding has limitations. It doesn't work on newly-summoned demons, only those that were in the hellhole when it got 'spiked'. It blasts the demons' minds, rendering them feeble-minded and confused for the most part. And it's magically destructive—spiking a hellhole causes tremendous arcane feedback that threatens to overload the Archmage's wards and disrupt other spells.

If the Crusader's plan is to use the same technique on the dozens of hellholes in Hellmarsh, the ensuing magical feedback may do more damage than any scheme of the Diabolist.

THIRTEEN RUMORS OF FIRST TRIUMPH

1: The road between Axis and Forge is now so beset by demons, bandits and orcs that the Emperor must take action soon. Everyone knows that the Crusader is the only force strong enough to protect the Empire's western flank. Soon, the road will be under our control.

2: The Crusader isn't the fist of the dark gods—they're *his* weapon. When the demons are destroyed, he'll turn on the dark gods and destroy them too. Step by step, campaign by campaign, he'll purge evil from the world and usher in the Age of Mortals. Every god, light and dark, will perish.

3: The Crusader is the true heir to the Empire—blessed by the Lich King, not the Emperor! The Lich King was the Wizard King of old, and one of his accomplishments was driving back the demons and building the first wards. Where did you think the Crusader's secret magic came from? No, one day the Crusader will be Prince of the Living, second only to the King of the Dead. Just ask the ghouls down in the Harvester Deeps, and they'll tell you the truth.

4: Burnt-out demon spirits get rehoused in the shells of war-golems. That's why they're so good at fighting—they don't know it, but they're really demons on the inside. If you talk to them for long enough, you might wake them up.

5: The Crusader's teachings burn mercy from our hearts. The Crusader's collecting the ashes of our pity, and from them he'll forge a new god, neither dark nor light, but divinely human. Only someone stole half the ashes. No doubt it was one of the Priestess' self-righteous holy thieves.

6: The Prince of Shadows has his spies and agents down in the Muster and Truth, fencing loot and stolen goods from lands conquered by the Crusader. If you want a good price for stolen goods, go down to the fourth sublevel and look for the room with a green door.

7: There are temples down in the Dark Temple to dead gods, ones that haven't been worshipped in Ages. Who built them, and why does the Crusader want them in his fortress? I'll tell you—the demons destroyed those gods and dragged 'em off to hell. One of these days, though, the Crusader's expeditions into the Abyss is going to find one of those dead gods. They'll drag its holy carcass back to First Triumph, and bring it back to life with all those stored demon essences! Can you imagine what the Crusader will do with a god that owes him a life debt?

8: First Triumph and the other hellholes held by the Crusader are on the western side of the Empire, west of Axis. Everyone thinks that the Crusader's going to march north to Hellmarsh next, but he's really looking to the east. Once he has a seaport and a navy, he'll be able to battle demons anywhere in the Empire. He's looking to Glitterhaegen... and if there's no hellhole there to give him an excuse to conquer the city and its port, why, he can make one!

9: Don't listen to her! The Crusader wants to build a navy so he can sail east, out through the Koru Straits and into the Iron Sea. Those behemoths that keep crawling out of the ocean and attacking the Empire—they're demons. There's a hellhole out there that makes the Abyss look like a kobold's nostril. Conquer that, and the Diabolist will be quaking in her evil slippers.

10: The other cities—Axis, Horizon, Glitterhaegen, New Port, even Concord—they've been quietly getting rid of all their beggars, lunatics, criminals and other undesirables by shipping them off to First Triumph. Ever wonder why the new recruits start off crazy, instead of going mad while they're here like we all did?

11: There isn't any Crusader. It's just a suit of armor, an idea. It's really the Archmage and the Emperor running the show. They know how bad things are going to get, but don't want to panic people. So, they've conjured up this puppet, this caricature of the bad knight, to do all the dirty things that need to be done.

12: So, the Great Gold Wyrm, the great enemy of the demons, falls into the Abyss—and suddenly, out of nowhere, there arises this invincible demon-hating warrior with incredible charisma and awesome magical powers? Do I have to draw you a diagram?

13: The end is coming! The end is coming! The end is coming!

CITADEL OF THE DIABOLIST

If the Diabolist wants you, her citadel will find you.

Like Archmage, High Druid, and Emperor, *Diabolist* is a title. There have been other Diabolists in the past; they perished of old age or violence or occult cataclysm, and in time a new Diabolist rose to claim the title. It's unclear, however, if one Diabolist significantly differs from the next.

The **Crusader** claims that the Diabolist is actually an evil spirit or demon that possesses the bodies of innocent women. Slay her, and she moves to another host that she then mutates into her preferred likeness.

Perhaps cryptic etchings in the archives of the **Dwarf King** suggest that the Diabolist is in thrall to her magical items! Certainly, she has a wealth of immensely potent items. How much of the Diabolist's behavior can be attributed to the war of spirits within her soul, as crown and staff and eye and ring pull her one way or the other?

The **Archmage** has concluded that the title of Diabolist comes with so many obligations and debts to the powers of Hell that anyone who claims it is trapped, like a spider caught in a web. He suspects that the Diabolist's occasional acts of mercy are all a good-hearted sorceress can manage.

According to rumors spread by the **Prince of Shadows**, the Diabolist was a human woman who, through sheer magical power, can will her own reincarnation. When slain, she is reborn somewhere in the Empire, and when she comes of age she returns to the Hell Marsh to reclaim her memories of her past lives and her mantle of power. Anyone, he whispers, could be the Diabolist in waiting. According to these tales, one of the main functions of the Diabolist's cult is to find and protect her when she is a young and vulnerable child.

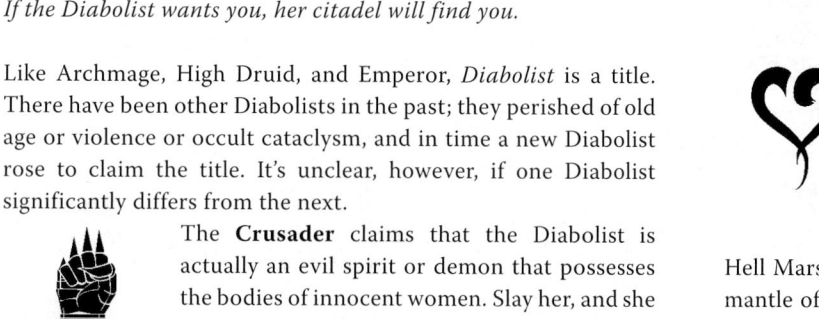

EIGHT VIEWS OF AN ICON'S STRONGHOLD

If the Diabolist isn't the queen of lies, it's not for lack of trying. She guards the truth in an avalanche of secrets. Her place of power in the Hell Marsh is no exception. Accounts of the fortress vary wildly in both appearance and location. Tales frequently put it somewhere in the center of the Hell Marsh, but it's been sighted as far east as the edge of the Queen's Wood, and as far south as the Kneedeep.

The only thing you can count on is that following Hell Marsh cultists (*Bestiary 2*, page 134), or listening to their stories, won't help you find it! Cultists relish helping to misdirect, and it seems to be a tenet of faith that no one should know where the Diabolist really is at any given time, unless she's right there in front of you. As to what the 'citadel' is . . .

"The boat took us from the Floating Market to a clearing deep in the swamp. There was a spiral staircase there, made of some reddish stone, warm to the touch, and it went down and down under the water. There was a labyrinth down there, with thousands of cells. Demons roamed the halls, and we were warned not to step outside our rooms. I didn't understand at first, but they brought me to one such cell. It was smaller than this one, with nothing there but a bed and a table and a chair, like a monk's room. There was a candle on the table.

Every morning, there'd be a knock on the door, and outside I'd find a tray with the day's food on it, and a fresh candle. Every day, I'd light that candle and stare into the flame, and I'd dream... or imagine... that she was talking to me, whispering secrets into my mind.

Nine years. Nine years I studied that candle. Nine years of secrets. That is why this cell holds no fear for me. I have transcended the needs of mortals... wait! Don't go! Don't leave me in the dark! Anything but the dark!"

—testimony of a demon cultist arrested in Forge

"On the twenty-seventh day, we found the lair of the fiend. It was a rotten finger of bone rising from the muck of the swamp, bathed in this hellish light. Demons of all kinds flocked around it, and laughed as the swamp vomited out blasts of burning gas. There were people there, too, hundreds of them, staggering blindly around in the mud. They were mad, all of them. I saw them shoveling mud and worms into their mouths and calling it a feast, drinking stagnant green water and thinking it wine, or shoving their faces into a patch of nettles and shouting that they'd learned occult secrets beyond imagining. Obviously, we ignored them and marched into the tower. It was full of traps and monsters, but our hearts were pure and our swords bright. We fought our way into the Diabolist's throne-room and killed her. She's dead. I killed her! Why are you looking at me like that? Why don't you believe me?"

—nameless human beggar, arrested in New Port for vagrancy

"Her citadel is a rose bush rooted in Hell, so large that its topmost blossoms are lost in the clouds. Through her magic, she has made delicate palaces of rosewater and crystal amid the thorns, and filled them with every imaginable delight. There are demons there, but you wouldn't know it— because they're not twisted and warped by having to compromise with base matter, they appear as they really are. They're beautiful, shining creatures, and so very kind. They taught me so much."

—Tengrian the Despoiler, awaiting execution by the Crusader's forces for murder and demon-worship

"My scrying spells have confirmed that the Diabolist has no citadel or home fortress, at least not in this incarnation. Instead, she has a roaming court or caravan of acolytes and demons that travel from hellhole to hellhole. In each hellhole, she maintains a tower or other small fortress, or demands shelter from a local demon lord. She never stays in one place for more than a few days.

Records from the end of the Twelfth Age are scarce—the Diabolist's plague threw the whole Empire into chaos. Stories of a 'tumult of the earth' and the 'breaking of the icons,' coupled with the recent discovery of the dungeon nicknamed the 'Devil's Grave' beyond Cairnwood, suggest to me that the previous Diabolist was slain by another icon, perhaps the vanished Swordmaiden, and her old fortress was overthrown in the process. When a new Diabolist arose, she chose not to repeat the same mistakes as her predecessor and so keeps moving to stay ahead of her enemies—such as the Crusader.

In summation, more scrying and research is required to develop a reliable method of tracking and observing the Diabolist. Please find bound to this parchment a miser-sprite educated in all the costs and expenses of such research program..."

—from a grant proposal to the School of Divination in Horizon

"Aye, I know the Old Woman's house. I won't take you there, not for any price. It ain't that it's too dangerous—I know how to get around the snakes and the beasties—but she doesn't want you there, and I won't anger her. I've seen her castle. It's half-sunk into the swamp—what did she expect, building a big stone pile like that in this muck? Every year, it sinks down more. I heard tell that in my grandfather's day, she summoned up some really big demons and had them pull it out of the mire, but now it's sinking back down again. The place looks half-rotten, but there are lights in the upper towers, and great big demons like toads and bats hopping around outside. And there are all the folk hanging from the trees?

What, you didn't know about those? I don't know who they are—strangers from out the swamp, most of 'em. They come to the castle, and fall asleep, and she has her demons hang 'em from the trees, and the wasps build nests around 'em. Don't know if they's sleeping or dead, or something else.

There are live folk there too. Elves, mostly, or what look like elves. She takes a few of our children as servants every year. Some of them even come back."

—Gorm Bluetooth, swampfolk hunter

"It was like a tongue of flame, only it was also a tower. Like it was made from dancing flames, and inside it was all gold and velvet and white marble, like a palace of dreams, but still on fire. I wasn't burned. I could walk across the floors of fire, and dance in halls of flame. I wasn't burned, until I defied her."

—Estran, the Burned

Best Guesses

Consistency, it is said, is the hobgoblin of little minds. Still, it's better to stuff your skull with as many hobgoblins as you can fit rather than try to make sense of the Diabolist's fortress. Can it be assumed that there are a few elements that are present in all the tower's incarnations? Perhaps we should speak of elements "present in each of the Diabolist's many fortresses", or "things which appear to the majority of unlucky visitors."

 There is, for example, a library containing a great many books, staffed by eerily helpful imps.

 There is an audience chamber for visiting dignitaries from the Abyss, where the most potent and terrible demon lords can manifest in a binding circle capable of restraining a deity.

 There are shrines and temples where the Diabolist's half-mad cultists worship her. The Diabolist appears to consider most of these cults a little embarrassing, like over-enthusiastic puppies who can't help but love her, and occasionally have accidents on the floor. (A little pee, a little uncontrolled demon summoning…) There are other cults in which she takes a more direct role, but she hides them among the host of sycophants and lunatics who attend her.

 There's a complex apparatus, a thing of bubbling green liquids, glowing gemstones, and screaming skulls that is some sort of monitoring device. Does it tell the Diabolist when the infernal pressures are growing too great, and warn her to open a new hellhole as a sort of occult vent, relieving the threat to reality? Or does it tell her where the wall between the worlds grows thin, so she can punch through and spill more of Hell into the mortal world?

 There is a garden where strange flowers bloom, bigger than redwood trees, attended by demonic insects the size of elephants.

 There is a chess game played with living pieces, but half the tyrants and mad wizards in the world have one of those. What distinguishes the Diabolist's game is that she cheats with merry abandon, changing the rules at her whim and turning pawns into knights and demons.

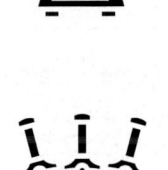 There is a little jetty where a black boat is moored. Step into this boat, and it'll sail you faster than the wind down a stream of night, and bring you to Shadowport—if you count the Prince of Shadows as a friend, that is.

There is, against all reason and logic, an apiary filled with tiny winged people instead of bees. Every hive has its own ruling icon, and they conduct little wars and intrigues against the hive across the aisle, military campaigns spanning nearly twenty feet of hard flying.

 There are torture chambers where crusaders and assassins who tried to destroy the Diabolist suffer eternally. Some of her demons are remarkably welcoming towards assassins, guiding them through the fortress and offering helpful tips about where to stab and what precautions to take. As no assassin has succeeded in slaying the Diabolist in this age of the world, either this is a tactic to throw intruders off-balance or an amusing diversion.

There are demons, of course. If the Diabolist's citadel is not actually in the Abyss, it is right on the threshold, and so all manner of demons dwell there. Unlike the Floating Market (p. 64), there are no universal rules or wards that protect visitors from the demons—if you're here, then either the Diabolist wants you here, or you're lunch.

Whims of the Diabolist

If you don't already have a scheme or three rolling yourself by the time the PCs reach the Diabolist's home turf, roll a d12 to see what she has decreed in her citadel today. If the players deserve it, roll a 13.

1: Revelry of Masks. Everyone must wear masks. Each mask is unique, and reveals something of the wearer's true personality and intent. The masks also place illusions around the wearers, dulling and hiding other physical attributes. It's not so much that you don't see that the woman in the mirror-mask is nine feet tall and bat-winged, it's just that didn't seem so important at the time.

2: War Eternal! Everyone in the citadel must kill someone else. You're safe once you've got blood on your hands.

3: She Walks Among You. The Diabolist has disguised herself as someone unremarkable—a serving girl, a cultist, a prisoner in the dungeons. If you find her and treat her kindly, she might be well disposed to you. If you scorn her, she will not be amused.

4: A Demon's Gift. Each demon is obliged to offer one gift or promise of service to a mortal in exchange for a token price. The mortal may suggest the price; the demon may refuse if it thinks the pay is too low, but the price may not exceed 10 gold pieces.

5: **Only Worship Will Do.** Everyone within the citadel knows that the Diabolist desires to be adored and worshipped, and fall over one another to be the most obsequious and servile. Those who show too much pride risk offending the icon.

6: **Time Shift.** Time in the Citadel flows very differently today. (Roll a d6—1: backwards, 2-3 too slow, 4-5 too fast 6 not at all).

7: **Forbidden Fruit.** Players may freely exchange up to one relationship die each for a positive relationship with the Diabolist.

8: **Merry-Go-Around.** The Citadel moves from one hellhole to another while the player characters are inside.

9: **Feast of Children.** There are far more children running around the Diabolist's halls than one might expect. Has she stolen them? Adopted them? Are they half-demons or changelings? Or are they some sort of tithe, offered by the fearful villages on the edge of the Hellmarsh to ward off the Diabolist's cruelty?

10: **Hearing of Petitions.** The Diabolist is willing to hear petitions this day. Her audience hall is crowded with diplomats, messengers and supplicants of all kinds, from the Empire and the mortal world. All requests will be given a hearing, at the very least; dull ones get fed to the giant vipers.

11: **Whispering Secrets.** Everyone in the Citadel hears whispering voices. Some plead for release or oblivion, others offer weird occult secrets and forbidden lore. At least one player character learns a secret he or she would prefer not to know.

12: **Mourning Day.** The Diabolist decrees that everyone in the Citadel must dress in mourning attire and accompany her on a pilgrimage to the tomb of one of the previous Diabolists, most of which are hidden in the choking depths of the Cairnwood.

13: **Tithed To Hell.** Even the Diabolist has debts to pay—and souls are the coin she must acquire. Every mortal in the Citadel is about to get hurled into the Abyss . . . .